Sophie Barat's Educational Vision

Marie-France Carreel

Translated by Constance Solari
Edited by Patricia C. Willis

ORIGINAL TITLE
SOPHIE BARAT: un projet éducatif pour aujourd'hui

Sophie Barat's Educational Vision
Marie-France Carreel
Translated by Constance Solari
Edited by Patricia C. Willis

Original Title:
SOPHIE BARAT: un projet éducatif pour aujourd'hui

Copyright © 2024 Society of the Sacred Heart. All rights reserved. No part of this book may be used or reproduced by any means, graphic, electronic, or mechanical, including photocopying, recording, taping or by any information storage retrieval system without the written permission of the editor except in the case of brief quotations embodied in articles and reviews.

Book design by Peggy Nehmen, n-kcreative.com

Printed in the United States of America
ISBN-13: 978-1-7364924-6-8 (paperback)

Published by:

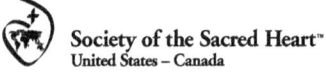

4120 Forest Park Avenue
St. Louis Missouri 63108-2809
314-652-1500
www.rscj.org

CONTENTS

Introduction 1

Part One: The Founding Educational Plan 5

Chapter I: The Provisional Plan of Study in Use at the House of Amiens 7

I.1   Beginnings 7
      Léonor de Tournély's Project 7
      Sophie Barat's Original Idea 11
      Joseph Varin, the Third Party Who Facilitated the Encounter 16
      The Boarding School at Amiens, Cradle of the Little Society 17

I.2   A Plan of Study Lost and Found 22
      The Unity of the *Plan of Study* 25
      A Well-Integrated Architecture 28
      The Program of Exercises of 1805 32
      Listening Carefully to the Divine Plan 36
      A Well-planned Course of Studies 39
      "In a Way That Is Familiar to Us" 44
      "Appropriate for Young Ladies" 48

Chapter II: Adoption of the Initial Plan 55

II.1   A Fomenter of Discord 56
      When Winds of Division Blow 56
      The Educational Plan of 1806 59
      The Plan of Studies of 1810 61
      Rules in Use within the Educational Community 64
      The Identity of the Founder 67

II.2   Confirmation of the Initial Decisions 73
      To Discover the Love of the Heart of Christ 74

"By All the Means within Their Power" 75
When Uniformity is Present at the General Council 79
The Hôtel Biron, Future "Fashionable Convent" 85
The Plan of Study is "Excellent" 87
In the Footsteps of Saint Francis Xavier 91
Except for What Does Not Agree with the Council of Trent 93
An Evocation of Origins 98

Chapter III: The Distinctive Educational Purpose of the Society of the Sacred Heart 105

III.1 In the Ignatian Tradition of Educational Congregations 105

Adapting to the Time and Place 105
Diversified Scholarly Recruitment 108
Christ Alive in the Faces of the Poor 111
When Intelligence and Compassion Go Hand in Hand 112
The Educational Model of Pierre Fourier 114
Appropriate for Day Students 116
The Plan of Studies Is Recommended to Other Institutes 124

III. 2 In Imitation of the Heart of Christ 127

Simplicity to Be Safeguarded 127
With Honesty, in the Image of Our Lady 129
When Decorum Pairs with Modesty 132
With Generosity, Beyond the Frontiers 135
From the Foundation to the Vatican II Council 142

Part Two: Toward the Accomplishment of the Founding Intuitions 145

Chapter I: The Post-Conciliar Updating of the Original Project 147

I. 1 Enlarging the Educational Space 148

From Separation to Presence 148

	The Missionary Framework for These Contacts	149
	Education, a Place for Revealing the Love of Christ	150
	A New Reference, the Rights of Man	152
	Daughters of the Church and Daughters of the Enlightenment	153
	New Vectors, Dialogue, and Collaboration	155
	A Demand for Justice Linked to Love	156
I.2	Differing Receptions of the New Orientations	160
	Evoking a Figure: Philippine Duchesne	160
	When the Model Shatters the Image	163
	When Departure is Rebirth	164
	A Great Cry, That of the Poor	166
	When Contrary Winds Blow	168
	Solidarity "from Within"	172
I.3	An Educational Program Introduced in the United States of America	174
	Contemporary Distinctiveness of the Schools of the Sacred Heart	175
	The Goals and Criteria	176

Chapter II: When the Metaphor of the River Comes to Life		187
II.1	Toward the River Whose Source Is in the East	188
	When Poverty Is Synonymous with Hope	189
	Return to the Source	190
	Water that Flows from the Source	194
	The River That Runs through History	196
II.2	The Collective Interpretation of the Original Educational Goals	198
	A Shifting of the Symbolic	200
	A Well-Ordered Decision-Making Process	201

	"Education for Justice in Faith"	206
	To Recognize the Presence of the Living God	209
	New Wineskins for New Wine	212

Chapter III: Constitutive Principles of Education in the Society of the Sacred Heart 217

III.1	Respect, the Place Where Encounter Can Occur	218
	At the Beginning, a *Presence*	218
	Awakeners of Meaning	221
	Gratuity as Golden Rule	222
	A Hope of Communicating to All Nations	227
III.2	A Pathway, to Discern in Order to Accomplish Justice	231
	Learning to Discern with a View toward Commitment	232
	To Walk Humbly, Making a Path Together	236
III.3	In Memory of the Covenant	238
	When Renewal is Accomplishment	239
	An Open Table	241

Conclusion: New Challenges, Living Water to Be Shared 247

Bibilography 251

Introduction

Sophie Barat
An Educational Project for Today

MANY OF OUR CONTEMPORARIES are seeking wisdom without knowing where or how to find it. Some search for a spirituality that responds to their thirst for interiority and compassion. Others despair of ever finding a place where solidarity is lived, somewhere they might find partners to promote such solidarity in a world where competition and profit are king. Educators today are expressing the need for a philosophy of education that gives meaning to the scholastic endeavor—that teaches students to orient themselves within the overwhelming crush of daily information and to discern between and among many conflicting opinions. In each case, the central issue is to restore the importance of the values that must underpin such choices, to educate with a view toward preventing violence in the cities, to know how to construct with others a future that is worthy of the human being.

This book represents a modest response to these goals. It proposes a way forward: Transcendence is Presence, discreet and active. As in the case of those on the road to Emmaus, it is at our side and shows itself available to all who invite it to their table. In short, beyond all of the reductive ideologies and supposed "horizontal" wisdoms of today, this text is witness to a collective experience: it recalls the power of the educational patrimony of the Society of the Sacred Heart. Herald of a spiritual tradition, it nevertheless displays a stunning modernity: Christ resurrected can liberate us all at the innermost place of our being and render us capable, in turn, of an infinite goodness.

As educators, we are called to prepare young people for this encounter with Christ, to give them the means to recognize his Presence and his Face in those who surround them. We must also show them how to travel the road with him in order to "accomplish a perfect justice."

This narrative is addressed to all people, young and not so young, who seek meaning, humanism, and evangelical authenticity. In a larger sense, it invites the reader living in this world of constant change to be inventive with respect to a common source.

At the moment I began this writing, I had a sudden memory of a special show of Cezanne's paintings of Mont Sainte-Victoire at the Petit Palais in Paris. The dynamic of the creative image was powerfully suggested in this exhibition. At the entry to the exhibition, the first paintings evoked its birth; in the center were ones that offered a view of sharp lines and warm colors; beyond these were two canvases that presented a sort of explosion and irradiation of the image. This deployment of a creative inspiration is not without analogy to the evolution of the foundational intuitions of the Society of the Sacred Heart at two key moments in its history: the foundation of the Society, realized between the years 1800 and 1827, and the renewal of the educational mission undertaken in response to the Second Vatican Council. For this reason, this book is articulated in two separate parts entitled *The Foundational Educative Plan* and *Toward the Accomplishment of the Initial Intuitions*.

After 1967, the Society of the Sacred Heart undertook a rapid change of its educational mission. Until then, its visibility and reputation brought to mind boarding schools for young girls and university prep schools; from this moment on, the Society opened itself to various forms of educational activity. The Conference of Latin American Bishops in 1968 in Medellín surfaced an international challenge: to recognize the injustice that underpinned the cry of the poor, whose dignity and basic rights were being outraged. The interpretation of the Society's original intuitions began to work alongside what was at stake internationally. And when the founding symbol of the Institute rediscovered its biblical roots, the metaphor of a river of living water expressed itself through a new set of images.

In order to appreciate this post-conciliar adaptation, it behooves us to understand the special educational features of the Society of the Sacred Heart at the moment of its founding. *The Founding Educational Plan* (Part I) proceeds to identify the style of education put in place by Sophie Barat. Comparative studies define both the tradition within which the initial project was maintained—and its novelty. *The Provisional Plan of Study in Use at the Amiens School* (Chapter 1) sketches the outlines of the founding intuitions and exposes the novelty of the first Plan of Study. Reflection, sometimes narrative, is based on historical critique, without limiting itself to this interpretive field because it also takes in accounts of foundation. *The Adoption of the*

Initial Plan (Chapter 2) evokes the difficulties undergone and their consequences for the established educational style; the dynamics of the growth realized between 1801 and 1826; and the confirmation of the initial choices. *The Special Educational Purposes of the Society of the Sacred Heart* (Chapter 3) clarifies the mission with respect to other feminine Ignatian traditions. The inspirational model is thus identified.

Toward the Accomplishing of the Initial Intuitions (Part II) is a rereading of the collective interpretation of the foundational project, undertaken between 1967 and 1982. *The Post-Conciliar Updating of the Initial Project* (Chapter 1) retraces the first steps forward and the obstacles encountered. *When the Metaphor of the River Makes Itself Known* (Chapter 2) recounts the shifting sense of the symbolism of the Heart of Christ and an interpretation of the initial aims. *The Constitutive Principles of Education in the Society of the Sacred Heart* (Chapter 3) are exposed in a final sketch, which presents how the philosophy of education is founded on the spirituality of the Institute.

The intervening history (one hundred and fifty years) would demonstrate how this evolution has taken place in interaction with the educational systems of different countries. But such a history would go beyond the limits of this study, which intends to demonstrate how the post-conciliar changes have become reality with respect to the original educational project. As both an analyst and a witness to these pages of recent history, I have had to impose a certain distance. I have done so by means of a critical approach—that of the philosophy of education—which aims to impart evangelical values, a source of synergy and institutional creativity.

PART ONE
The Founding Educational Plan

CHAPTER I

The Provisional Plan of Study in Use at the House of Amiens

I.1 Beginnings

THIS INTRODUCTORY SECTION PROPOSES to make clear the earliest expression given by Léonor de Tournély and Sophie Barat to the service of education of the Society of the Sacred Heart—to define its contours. Two texts relay this earliest plan: the project of Léonor de Tournély and the creative inspiration of Sophie Barat, or the "primordial idea of the little Society."

Study of this history will allow us to see the portrayals, the images, and the integral values of the culture of the Society of the Sacred Heart at the time of its foundation. It will allow us to see how the educational aims were organized around a founding symbol.

Léonor de Tournély's Project
Ordained a priest at the Parisian seminary of Saint-Sulpice, under the direction of Monsieur Emery, Léonor de Tournély took refuge in Antwerp at the time of the French Revolution.

In 1794, with Charles de Broglie, he founded a society of priests that took as its model the Society of Jesus. Their intent was to follow in the footsteps of Ignatius Loyola. The name of the new order was "The Company of the Heart of Jesus."

Pursued by the revolutionary army, this first group of priests fled to Holland. Forced to move on to Germany in July 1794, in the border town of Venloo, they were joined by Joseph Varin, a former Sulpician seminarian now attached to the army of the counter-revolutionary Prince de Condé. But Father de Tournély guessed that this new Society represented only one aspect of the remedy for the social emptiness caused by the revolutionary turmoil. He also dreamed of founding a society of women, devoted to the Sacred Heart of Jesus and having the same educational goals with respect to young women. One of his associates, Fidèle de Grivel, wrote: "In the month of January 1796, Father de Tournély was, in his prayers, consumed by two ideas. The first was to go to Rome and fulfill his vow of October 14, 1794 (to put himself at the pope's disposal). The second was to form an order of women, according to the Constitutions of Saint Ignatius, but adapted to their sex; these women would occupy themselves with education and with the care of the sick, but within the cloister, somewhat like the Elisabethines of Vienna."[1] Such an adaptation would include modification of the rules of enclosure imposed by canon law according to the Council of Trent.

In 1796, the winds of revolution had systematically destroyed the French convents, considered to be bastions of the *Ancien Régime*. Léonor de Tournély was well aware of this

---

1   *Breve Ragguaglio*, 18. Cited by J. de Charry, *Histoire des Constitutions de la Société du Sacré-Coeur*, Première Partie, La Formation de l'Institut, Exposé historique, Vol. 1, 1ère édition, Rome, 1975, A.S-C. F, p. 120.

situation: current social and political circumstances called for an institutional format that differed from the convents of old. His idea for a future institute brought together missionary daring, prudent judgment, and a clear sense of realism. Without wishing to derogate canon law, he opted quite deliberately for an apostolic mission in which the society members' visibility and participation within the larger society were different from those of the *Ancien Regime*. In order to better suggest this idea, he had recourse to two comparisons: "rather like the Elisabethines of Vienna" or "like the Sisters of Charity." He did not call upon the model of the former educational monasteries.

The allusion to the Sisters of Charity is particularly significant. Their founder, Saint Vincent de Paul, had in his own way chipped away at the canonical rule of enclosure. Father de Tournély may have seemed not to think about it, but his intention to make such an adaptation was clear. For a congregation envisioned along the lines of the Society of Jesus, with a central government and an exchange of personnel among houses, the rule of papal enclosure[2] would pose enormous difficulties. In 1607, the *Company of Our Lady* of Jeanne de Lestonnac had experienced such difficulties; in 1717, the Institute founded by Mary Ward suffered the same fate. The Constitutions of the *Company of Our Lady* or those of Saint Ursula showed what obstacles educational monasteries had to overcome in order to receive day students into their classrooms. The minutiae of the regulation, the endless recourse to the bundles of keys, and the regulation of movement and gesture lent the establishment a surreal image of a claustrophobic universe that bordered on

---

[2] It is called "papal enclosure" because only authorization by the pope could allow an exception to the rule.

imprisonment. While wishing to maintain an environment that was relatively conventual, Léonor de Tournély chose a new way of interacting with that environment. The project's innovation also took from the Ignatian model a variety of approaches to such an undertaking.

However, at the end of the eighteenth century, the social status of women opened the door to a very limited field of operations: teaching and nursing Moreover, "what is suitable" for women at a given time can evolve a century or two later, when their social status has changed substantially. The notion of "suitability" thus brings with it a historical and cultural relativity, and it indicates a capacity for openness and subsequent transformations. If the diversity of religious women's ways of engaging with the world did not become fully realized until Vatican II and the suppression of conventual cloister, Tournély's initial plan showed that it was possible. His women's order was based on the Ignatian model, which opened the definition of apostolic work to many possibilities, patterned on the ultimate goal of the Institute.

An anecdote serves to set his project in his time. In 1795, after a severe winter that brought with it hardships concerning food and shelter, members of the community of the Fathers of the Sacred Heart fell ill. Léonor de Tournély hired a religious *emigrée* by the name of Sister Scholastica, based on her qualifications as a nurse. However, states Fidèle de Grivel with a note of humor, this person "did nothing but make us practice patience and failed to heal anyone." But in listening to her ideas, Léonor de Tournély thought of founding a new order of women. Several members of the community were consulted and the project was approved.

While this anecdote might well seem amusing, it provides a basis for the origin story. It has interest for us because it preserves the ordinariness of the everyday that is too often overtaken by the realm of the sacred. Moreover, the impact of concrete reality, together with communal discernment, gives an Ignatian quality to the decision-making process. Through communal deliberation, an idea became a project assumed over the long term by an entire group. The order of women would be consecrated to the Sacred Heart of Jesus, whose devotion it would spread. It would be apostolic, that is to say following the Ignatian model, from which it would also adopt its Constitutions and its rules.

We must now consider Sophie Barat's creative inspiration. Does it in fact constitute a comparable idea? And in what context did it come to her?

Sophie Barat's Original Idea

Madeleine Sophie Barat was born on December 12, 1779, in the rue du Puits Chardon in the town of Joigny, along the Yonne River. Third child of Jacques Barat, barrel-maker and vintner, and Marie-Madeleine Fouffé, she was born prematurely. Small in stature, effervescent in wit and intelligence, Sophie was already, at the age of seven, the pupil of her brother Louis—a student at the major seminary of Sens, then run by the Abbé François Montant. At the age of nine, she began her study of Latin. At the time a teacher at the *Collège Saint-Jacques* in Joigny, her brother took her through the stages of a thorough education in the Humanities. At his insistence, she completed the same assignments as his male students at Saint-Jacques, as later recalled by a former student's memory of Louis: "Have you no shame, boys, [Father Barat exclaimed] that it is a young woman who is at the top of our class in Greek?"[3] Sophie received a solid basic education. At the same time, she learned the dressmaker's trade.

In 1790, Louis was sent to Paris to complete his education. While a student at the *Collège des Quatre Nations,* he followed the courses of Fourcroy, Jussieu and Daubenton. To the study of natural sciences, chemistry, and mathematics (which he particularly relished), he added foreign languages. He subsequently returned to Joigny, to the *Collège Saint-Jacques,* just as the Terror was beginning. Upon the order of Cardinal Loménie de Brienne, his archbishop, he swore loyalty to the Civil Constitution of the Clergy[4] in January 1791, but retracted his oath in June 1792. Pursued by the municipal police, he fled to Paris. Captured there, he was imprisoned, barely escaped the guillotine, and was liberated in January 1795. He then became a clandestine priest. After a great deal of hesitation, his parents consented to let his sister join him in Paris. He introduced her to biblical studies, theology and patristics, as well as the study of Hebrew. Under his severe direction, Sophie acquired an intellectual formation of the highest caliber, exceptional for a young woman of her age and milieu.

It was during this Parisian interlude that she experienced the intuition of what she called "the original idea of our little Society." The story of this spiritual experience was written by a religious of the Institute, Pauline Perdrau. It is impossible to date this critical experience, but the end of Pauline Perdrau's

---

3   Cited by M-J. Vié, *Louis Barat, Le frère de Sainte Madeleine-Sophie, 1768-1845,* A. S-C.F., 2000, p. 12.

4   Ordained to the sub-diaconate in 1789 and professor at the *Collège* at Joigny, Louis Barat was required by the government to take this oath.

story indicates that it happened just before the first meeting between Sophie and Joseph Varin.[5]

This account begins as follows: "I remember our Holy Mother speaking of something truly remarkable, and I don't find reference to it in what has been written about her, a fact that gives me the task of writing it down as I heard it." Then, as background, Perdrau relates the post-revolutionary context. She describes the behavior of Christians, characterized by a faithful attachment to Christ, the importance of adoration of the Blessed Sacrament and solidarity around one central objective: to raise the awareness of families to the active presence of Christ in their daily lives. The tableau she paints strikingly suggests Sophie's surroundings—her work as a dressmaker and her attraction to the spiritual.

Next, Perdrau relates the spiritual experience that gave rise to the *original idea of the little Society* first presented itself to Sophie. The account is given in two temporal stages: a "before" and an "after." This burst of creative intuition is signified by several ellipses. Below is a schematic representation:

before: the social and ecclesial context— a first project for religious life	Creative Intuition: the original idea of the little Society	after: the future takes on a new orientation

---

5 "And it was animated by these dispositions that Father Varin found her, even as he was seeking—as I will indicate later—this foundational rock predicted by Father Tournély." Pauline Perdrau, *Les Loisirs de l'Abbaye*, Volume 1, Rome, 1936, A.S-C. F, p. 424.

The first stage is expressed thus: "So here I was with this original idea of our little Society of the Sacred Heart, that of uniting myself with other young women in order to establish a small community which, night and day, would adore the Heart of Jesus that had been outraged in its Eucharistic love."

Then Sophie seems to move away from her original plan, prompted by the desire to listen to the needs around her. "But, I said to myself, when we are twenty-four nuns replacing each other on the prie-Dieu in order to accomplish the task of perpetual adoration, this will offer both a great deal and a very little towards accomplishing our noble task. . . . " And an intuition intervened. Within a short time, a lifetime project morphed from one shape into another. Young Sophie, until then attracted to life as a Carmelite, where she could devote herself exclusively to adoration and reparation, allowed herself to be moved by the crises in society and in the Church of her time. She imagined at that moment consecrating herself to education. And this is the second phase of the experience: a future was opening before her.

If we had young girls whom we formed in the spirit of adoration and reparation, how different that would be! And I saw hundreds, thousands of adorers before an ideal, universal monstrance, lifted up over the Church. This is it, I said to myself, before a solitary tabernacle: we must dedicate ourselves to the education of the young, develop in their souls the solid foundations of lively faith in the most blessed Sacrament, and thus combat those traces of Jansenism that have led to godlessness, and with the revelations of Jesus to Blessed Margaret Mary on the reparative and expiatory devotion to his Sacred Heart in the most blessed Sacrament, we will raise up a crowd of adorers in every country, to the ends of the world.

The transformation enabled by Eucharistic adoration was integral to Sophie's spiritual experience and thus, in this sense, to her charism. The energy that emanated from such adoration was the basis of her ardor: to communicate an existential meaning to the youth of a society marked by an ethical vacuum that followed from revolutionary turmoil. Sophie's spiritual plan was the result: "to form young women of all nations in the spirit of adoration and reparation." Sophie wanted to pass on that which she herself had discovered: the power of liberation and the compassion of the Heart of Jesus. And the best method she found to accomplish this was to educate young women in a way that—through their contemplation of Christ, the very "center and model" of any evangelical life—would allow them to become the leavening agent within a societal transformation, in the service of the dignity of the human person, created in the image of God. "To refashion in their souls the solid foundation offered by a lively faith"—such was her goal, right from the very beginning, outlining a missionary dimension and a globalization of the enterprise.

Contrary to the project envisioned by Léonor de Tournély, this creative inspiration did not specify the legal form of the future educational community. Rather, the missionary dimension itself was further specified. Thus, one might say that each expression offers a specific contribution: that of Léonor de Tournély offers an apostolic model and a social purpose; that of Sophie Barat focusses more on a missionary dynamic. These two ideas characterize the beginning of the Institute. The element they share is the symbol of the Heart of Christ, the frame of reference for the original plan. The Good News to be communicated is the "new" Life, offered at any moment, flowing from the open side of the risen Christ.

But how were these two creative inspirations to be joined in one work?

Joseph Varin, the Third Party Who Facilitated the Encounter

In 1797, Joseph Varin succeeded Léonor de Tournély as superior general of the Fathers of the Sacred Heart. It was incumbent upon him to bring to fruition the project of his predecessor. However, on April 18, 1799, the Society of the Fathers of the Sacred Heart joined with the Fathers of the Faith, whose superior general was Niccolò Paccanari. On May 31, 1799, Paccanari founded in Rome a women's branch of this order called the *Dilette di Gesù*. Léopoldine Naudet was the superior general.

During the summer of 1800, Joseph Varin was sent to France to found a house of the Fathers of the Faith and a corresponding society of women. Soon after his arrival in Paris, he made the acquaintance of Sophie Barat, with her brother Louis serving as go-between. The founding "event" of the Society of the Sacred Heart of Jesus flows from the dynamism of this meeting when the call to missionary work took hold. But the priority of Sophie's project is interesting in several ways. It demonstrates that the young woman had chosen to be an educator. And it provides information on the symbolic significance of this meeting where the mutual importance of a personal call and an undertaking for the Church was first recognized.

Thus, on November 21, 1800, in the apartment of one Mlle Duval in Paris's rue de Touraine, Sophie consecrated herself to the religious life along with three other young women. This commitment is considered the founding moment of the Institute.⁶ During the year 1800-1801, these four women learned the ways of religious life, under the supervision of Father Varin. For Geneviève Deshayes, "that is where the true foundations of the Society of the Sacred Heart were laid, a spirit that was broad, strong, generous, but completely infused with gentleness, dauntlessness, strength, leniency: this is what our dear Sophie and her companions tried hard to acquire in this place of recollection and solitude."⁷

The Boarding School at Amiens, Cradle of the Little Society

In the autumn of 1801, the first boarding school opened in Amiens in the rue Martin Bleu-Dieu. The legal transfer of Mlle Devaux's secular institute was signed on October 15, and on November 13, the first religious were brought together. Mlles Geneviève Deshayes and Henriette Grosier joined them. The community took the name "The Ladies of Christian Instruction" because "Sacred Heart" was a term still forbidden them.⁸ Life began to come together. Mlle Loquet, the director of the boarding school, was named superior. Geneviève Deshayes was responsible for the lower grades, and Marguerite, Mlle Duval's former maid, for the manual labor. Sophie was charged with the upper grades, where she also taught religion. A remark of Adèle

---

6   The identification of a founding event within a religious congregation always occurs after the fact because it surfaces a collective consensus. As an act of recognition, it is a constitutive part of the process of foundation. See C. Langlois, *Le catholicisme au féminine, Les Congrégations françaises à supérieure générale au XIX siècle*, Deuxième partie, Ch. IV, Cerf, 1984, p. 160.

7   Autobiographical notes of G. Deshayes, AGSS-C, A II, p. 10.

8   At the end of the eighteenth century, to bear the name *Sacred Heart* signified adherence to that branch of the French Church that opposed both the Jansenist current and the anti-religious polemic of the Enlightenment.

Cahier attests to the influence she exerted on her students: "Several distinguished families hurried to entrust their daughters to the new teachers. Princess Amélie de Berghes was one of those who received the direct attention of Mother Barat. Even though she was only eleven or twelve at the time, the child was struck by the rare qualities of her mistress, while the princess, her mother, was surprised to find in her relations with the young religious such tact and such a graceful familiarity with the way in which things were done properly—a familiarity that many never develop over a lifetime."[9]

The school's reputation spread quickly in the city. Beginning in the month of February 1802, a day school was opened. Six months later, the number of day students had risen to 165, a considerable number for that era; enrollment at the boarding school grew from twenty to forty students. They were eventually forced to find a new location on the other side of the city, in the rue Neuve. The boarders were primarily from families of the bourgeoisie, though there were a few from the aristocracy. The recruitment of students corresponded to the vision of Léonor de Tournély. At the beginning of the nineteenth century, the image of society more or less consciously echoed that of the *Ancien* Régime: a hierarchical society, in which the social classes occupied positions that corresponded to their respective rank. Its chief value was that of order, a value not swept away by the French Revolution, and on some level even reinforced by the Enlightenment.

In the ecclesiastical world, this vision of society was bolstered by a concept of salvation according to which the poor,

---

9   A. Cahier, *Vie de la Vénérable Mère Barat*, Tome I, Ch. VI, E. de Soye et Fils, Paris, 1884, A. S-C. F., p. 75.

having suffered hardships "here below" that were often extreme, would find happiness in the "next world." The essential thing was to prepare them for eternal salvation, but under no circumstances to allow them to escape their poverty or their difficult conditions. On the other hand, the wealthy, benefiting from an elevated social position, had to assure their own salvation by leading a virtuous life. It was thus extremely important to take care of their education and, down the line, that of the mothers of the future.

Passed on by Christian families during the seventeenth and eighteenth centuries, this idea endured and brought with it a selection of scholarly pursuits. "During the nineteenth century, girls of the leisured class did not generally attend schools designed for the general population. If, along with 'rich' boarding students, a convent admitted 'poor' day students, care was taken that the two classes were not schooled together. This segregation introduced another type during the same period: (…) the young women would not all be instructed in the same way."[10] For the boarding school, this was considered the best educational formula, in the sense that it kept a young woman safe from harmful influences until she could make her own choices, assert herself, and develop her own sense of discernment.

At the end of the year 1802, Mlle Loquet left the Institute with the consent of Louise Naudet, who had come from Rome to visit the new community. On December 21, the young Sophie was named local superior. To help her in her new responsibilities, Joseph Varin, ecclesiastical superior, named Father Bruson, director of the *collège* for young men, and Father Sambucy de

---

10 F. Mayeur, *L'éducation des Filles au XIXe siècle*, Hachette, Le temps et les hommes, 1979, p. 9.

Saint-Estève, a priest who had recently joined the Fathers of the Faith. To Father Loriquet, he entrusted the supervision of studies and the training of teachers.[11] A decision was made to relieve Sophie Barat of her teaching duties. At the end of 1803, Geneviève Deshayes was named mistress general of the boarding school and Anne Baudemont, the assistant to the superior.

The year 1804 was marked by two major events. The first was the separation of the Amiens community from the Institute of the *Dilette di Gesù* in Rome, which remained under the jurisdiction of Paccanari. This happened following the decision taken by Joseph Varin to leave Paccanari's association on June 21, 1804. The second event was the departure of Sophie Barat, on November 22, to oversee a new foundation in Grenoble. When Father Varin presented this project to her, he added: "You will find there several people, but one above all—even if she were the only one and placed on the other side of the world—you would have to seek out." This person was Philippine Duchesne.

Philippine Duchesne was born in Grenoble on the 29th of August, 1769, to a family of the financial and political *haute bourgeoisie*; she was the second of eight children born to Pierre-François Duchesne, a lawyer influenced by the spirit of the Enlightenment, and Rose-Euphrosine Périer, whose family was

---

11 J.-N. Loriquet, born August 5, 1767, in Epernay (Marne), Master of Arts at the University of Reims, graduate of the Seminary of Saint-Sulpice, was ordained a deacon in 1790. He joined the Fathers of the Faith in Amiens in 1802. This expert in pedagogy was professor of the highest class and dean of studies at the school. Between 1803 and 1805, twice a week, he oversaw the formation of the classroom teachers. When the Jesuits were reinstated in 1814, he was received by Father de Clorivière and made his first vows at Montmorillon on July 31, 1816. In October of the same year, he was sent to be superior at the *Collège de Saint-Acheul* in Amiens. He died in Paris on April 9, 1845.

the proprietor of the Château de Vizille. Philippine benefited from the same primary education given to her cousins, one of whom, Casimir Périer, would become Prime Minister during the July Monarchy.[12] At an early age, Philippine was captivated by the stories of the missionaries. She eventually became a boarding student with the Visitation nuns at Sainte-Marie d'En Haut in Grenoble. Her fierce desire to become a religious flew in the face of her parents' categorical refusal. She pretended to submit to them, but in 1787, without the consent of her father, she entered the Visitation novitiate. Monsieur Duchesne finally gave in to his daughter's stubbornness, but in September 1789, predicting the oncoming revolutionary persecutions, he forbade her to pronounce her final vows.

In fact, in September 1792 the community of Sainte-Marie d'En-Haut was forced to disperse, and in April of the following year, the abandoned monastery was turned into a prison. Returned to Grenoble at the height of the Terror, Philippine created an association, "Ladies of Mercy," whose goal was to restructure a religious life devoted to the education of children, and whose specific purpose was to administer to the social needs of the poor and abandoned. She also visited those who were dying or in prison. In 1801, with the financial help of her family, she undertook the reopening of Sainte-Marie d'En-Haut, tried without success to reassemble her old community, and dreamed of becoming a missionary in China. It was at this point that she asked to join the *Dames de l'Instruction Chrétienne*—the name then given to Sophie Barat's Institute.

---

12   Tr. note: The July Monarchy, also known as "the bourgeois monarchy," refers to the period between 1830 and 1848, during which a liberal constitutional monarchy was in place under King Louis Philippe.

Over the course of the 1804-5 school year, two documents were produced in Amiens: the *Provisional Plan of Study Used at the House of Amiens*[13] and the *Program of Exercises*. Their publication was simultaneous and represented both a measure of caution and a founding instrument of the initial educational plan.

I.2 A Plan of Study Lost and Found

The 1804 Plan of Study is a notebook of twenty-five manuscript pages. It is entitled:

**The Provisional Plan of Study
in Use at the House of Amiens**

Its dilapidated state speaks to the many times it was consulted and moved about. The cover is ripped, the color is faded, the pages are dog-eared. Other documents written on the same paper, dated from 1804 to 1806, have retained their original color, a pale blue-green. However, their existence had been ignored for many years. The gathering of original documents in one central archive in 1987 allowed me to discover it in April of 1989.

This fact redoubles our interest—one might even say our mandate—to identify its author and undertake a close study of it. For this analysis, we shall use the method recommended by François de Dainville: "to trace the origin of each item in order

---

13 In the manuscript, (A.G.S.C., D-I, 1) –a), the word "study" appears in the singular. For this reason and for purposes of this text, we have chosen to adhere to this spelling. The term refers simultaneously to the methods of study and the educational materials.

to discover its meaning."[14]

Jean-Nicolas Loriquet is the author of the *Plan of Study*: on the first page of the manuscript, in the upper left-hand corner, are the initials "A.M.D.G.,"[15] an acronym he used to sign his work. His biography refers to it in unequivocal terms:

> In 1804, Father Loriquet's experience was sought in writing a Plan of Study for the young women in the boarding school, in which his verses more than once helped to enable moments of piety or of gratitude. Among the books indicated as specific to each class, one discovers several that are marked with the cross and published by Rusand: *Lhomond's French Grammar*, revised and edited; *Summary of the Geography of Different Ages, etc.*; *Elements of Arithmetic*, etc.; *Chronological Table of Ancient and Modern History*, etc.; *Ecclesiastical History with Questions and Answers*, etc. These works are by the author of the *Plan of Study*, who remarked in a final note, dated October 5, 1804, "that the textbooks on ancient and Roman history are not yet published," and that "the one on the history of France has not yet been written."[16]

The document was thus composed several weeks before Sophie Barat's departure for the Grenoble foundation.

---

14   F. de Dainville, *La naissance de l'Humanisme moderne*, opening paragraph of the Preface, Slatkine Reprints, Geneva, 1969, p. IX.

15   *Ad Majorem Dei Gloriam*, To the greater glory of God.

16   A. Guidée, *Notice du R. Père Jean-Nicolas Loriquet,* Poussielgue-Rusand, Paris, 1845, AFSJ, p. 75.

Manuscript of first page of Plan of Studies of 1804.

The Unity of the *Plan of Study*
By way of introduction, one finds the following brief remark: "The success of a Plan of Study depends essentially on the allocation of time wisely managed, the arrangement of the lessons, and the style of teaching." These three elements recur throughout the text. The allocation of time is explained in chapters I through III. The style of instruction is developed in chapters IV through X. The class schedules are addressed throughout the document. The epigraph points to the component parts of the document.[17]

The seeming simplicity of the structure might be illustrated as follows:

Ch. I	art 1. ALLOCATION OF TIME (see the Rule for students) art 2. DIVISION OF CLASSES art 3. GOAL OF INSTRUCTION FOR EACH CLASS: (5th, 4th, 3rd, 2nd, 1st, Superior class)
Ch. II	ON ADMISSION INTO THE CLASSES
Ch. III	ALLOCATION OF TIME FOR EACH CLASS
Ch. IV	ON THE RECITATION OF LESSONS
Ch. V	ON THE CORRECTING OF HOMEWORK
Ch. VI	READING
Ch. VI	FRENCH GRAMMAR AND SPELLING
Ch. VII	ARITHMETIC
Ch. VIII	HISTORY
Ch. IX	GEOGRAPHY
Ch. X	LITERATURE

---

17 *Plan d'Étude provisoire à l'usage de la Maison d'Amiens.*

The document is held together by the inclusion of information on the length of time to be spent on studies. This idea is repeated in chapters I and X.

Chapter I is composed of three sections entitled, respectively: "Allocation of Time," "Division of Classes," "Goal of Instruction for Each Class." Integrating these elements, Jean Nicolas Loriquet points the way to a special area of education and defines it under these three headings. As if his gaze were playing rapidly across a building in order to define and name its architecture, he determines the essential elements of the educational system put in place between 1801 and 1804.

The first article, entitled "Allocation of Time," returns without any other commentary to the general Rule for students, whose first section lays out "the order of the lessons or the allocation of time" by day and by week, including the distinctive features of days of *congé*,[18] vacation, and exams. The general framework of life in the boarding school is given in ten scenarios, to establish *the schedules of different days*:

of each day	for days of home economics
of Sundays and ordinary feasts	specific to certain days
for days of ordinary congé	specific to each month
for feast days of special importance	specific to each trimester
for days of special congé	for days of annual congé.

Why did the author refer only to the general Rule if the rhythm of school life, "the order of day," is considered essential?

---

18   Tr. note: *Congé* is a French term for a holiday, time off, or break from studies. The term is still used in some Sacred Heart schools to designate a surprise break from the normal school day for games or other recreational activities.

The significance of this wording is revealed in the first lines of Article 2, entitled "Division of Classes," where the course of study is set forth. The designation "Course of Study" opens the presentation. This concept, focusing on several different terms (classes, courses, educational goals), is central to the design of the plan. The author is not composing an educational treatise like those in use during the eighteenth century, but a program of studies. Instruction is said to be a clear-cut option.

The third article of Chapter 1 confirms this goal. It spells out the program of teaching and defines a structure whose elements are adjusted by the linking of one academic class with another, for arithmetic, for example. In the fourth class, the following topics comprise a lesson: the system of counting, knowledge of Roman numerals, and the Rule of Four. In third class are added decimal and metric calculations, fractions, and the first three complex numbers. The second class considers complex division and geometric calculation. Finally, in the first class, students study the Rule of Three and bookkeeping. Other subjects follow the same kind of progression.

Chapter I of the *Plan of Study* for 1804 therefore defines an educational style based on instruction.

The subsequent chapters specify how to go about it:

- Chapter II gives the criteria for admission into the next level of the course of studies;
- Chapter III presents the order of scholastic lessons for each class, morning and evening;
- Chapters IV through X demonstrate a variety of teaching methods.

A Well-Integrated Architecture

Chapter II outlines the criteria for admission into the next academic class. The formula for doing so is as follows:

> The rules of grammar and spelling are the main goals of teaching for the classes. The level of progress in this area of the curriculum determines the class into which a student should be admitted, whatever her age or her progress in handwriting, history, etc. She cannot advance into the next class until she has shown a sufficient mastery over the rules of grammar taught in the preceding class.

Promotion to the next level, linked to this rule of admission, is applied solely to the French language program. Its strictly applied character is justified by its function: to guarantee discipline. The argument admits no exception: "This rule is necessary because it is the only means of preventing trouble and confusion within the course of study." No exceptions were made. To break this rule could harm the educational identity of a newly founded boarding school, as well as incur the risk of mediocrity in the development of students.

Chapter VI, on reading and the teaching of the French language, gives us the reasoning behind it: to be skilled in communicating well. But why does this chapter have the same numbering as the preceding chapter about reading? Is this a simple mistake, or does it have significance?

A glance at the reading exercises for the second and third classes reveals that this area of study has the same objective as the study of language. This is why the two articles have the same numbering and might be brought together under the same title: "reading and writing." At the end of their schooling, the boarding students were required to compose and recite "short speeches on subjects both instructive and amusing, always appropriate for the instilling of ideas that are proper, elegant and religious." That was the goal.

There are three steps in learning to read. The first corresponds to the fifth class, whose purpose is to upgrade reading and writing skills in preparation for admission into the fourth.[19] The students are divided into two groups. One serves the needs of "the students who do not know how to read at all and those who have great difficulty in doing so or who, not advanced enough, require private lessons." The second is composed of "other students whom one follows with special care." All of these students are given readers. Learning to read prepares students to study history lesson and then to commit it to memory.

The next stage applies to the fourth and third classes. Here, reading accompanies learning to write. Through reading, the students familiarize themselves with a text that they must then summarize in order to make it their own. Reading prepares the student analysis and synthesis.

A third stage characterizes the second and first classes. There is an important schedule change here: reading is limited to days of *congé*. At this level, it is expected to be enjoyable, relaxing, and cultural. In the second class, recitation helps the student to master pronunciation. And in the first, special care is taken to make sure that the reading is varied.

---

19 According to the admissions records at the boarding school, students in the fifth class were between eight and ten years old.

The three levels might be thus represented:

Level	Class	Program	Objectives
1	5th	Readers	to know how to read and write well enough to move into the 4th Class
2	4th	Book: ancient history (to be read 3 times)	to prepare them to write excerpts to prepare them to write summaries
2	3rd	Books: Roman history History of France	
3	2nd	Prose	to learn how to pronounce and recite well
3	1st	Poetry	to master clear elocution
3	1st	Manuscripts	to learn to decode all kinds of writing

The first objective, "to read easily and express oneself clearly," corresponds to the teaching of grammar and spelling, "to write correctly." This skill is acquired by means of a well-defined division of the program and the learning process:

Class	Objectives
5th	To learn to spell ordinary words
4th	To learn to distinguish the five parts of speech To learn to conjugate irregular verbs
3rd	To learn how to apply the rules for verbs and participles
2nd	To review the program of the 3rd class and to master the knowledge of the other parts of speech
1st	To reinforce mastery by reviewing the program of the 2nd class, focusing on the most difficult rules

Learning to spell is a longstanding concern. It was recommended by both Fénelon and Rollin. However, compared to his predecessors, Jean-Nicolas Loriquet did not limit the learning of grammar to its rudiments. He associated with it another objective: to develop the mind by means of understanding its rules, including dictionary definitions and genders. Just speaking well was not enough; students had to master the French language.

There are two levels of learning here: learning rules and discovering literature. This choice is specified in the first paragraph of chapter X: "Literature should not be approached by the students until they have a firm grasp of grammar and spelling, and know how to observe the rules of each, whether they are speaking or writing: this does not occur until the end of the third class."

Teaching promoted integrative learning in specific stages. The process was delineated in this way:
- in third class: letter-writing;
- in second class: history;
- in first class: poetry;
- in the superior class: oratory.

The mastery of French usage began with the learning of reading in the fifth class. Its goal was to master the rules of syntax, grammar and spelling in the fourth and third classes. In this way, the student could reach a new milestone: the study of poetry. To arrive at this level marks the passage into literary culture properly understood. The role of preparation—first given to reading in order to study history—is here assigned to reading poetry the gateway to literature. In the superior class,[20] the beginning study of rhetoric moves on to the rules of public speaking.

Thus, the regulations for moving from one class to the next provide consistency in the curriculum. Each stage of learning is directed toward the same goal: to enable the student to communicate with ease, simplicity and elegance. But to understand the levels of instruction, we must examine a second document, composed in 1805.

The Program of Exercises of 1805

This work was published at "Amiens, by J. Bapt CARON the elder, Publisher-Bookseller for His Excellency the Bishop, Place de la Concorde." It is entitled:

HOUSE OF INSTRUCTION
OF AMIENS,
Rue de l'Oratoire, N° 7.

*

PROGRAM
OF
THE VARIOUS EXERCISES
That will be undertaken by the Students, and followed by the
SOLEMN DISTRIBUTION OF PRIZES.

This document has nothing to do with a prize list or prospectus, but with a program of studies presenting the

---

20 Tr. note: The superior class followed the first class and consisted of a review of the student's previous studies, followed by rhetoric, natural history, and the fundamentals of faith.

concepts taught within each discipline for each academic class. The prize lists for the following years specify only the parts of the educational program; the theoretical account has disappeared. This document is therefore unique and permits us to appreciate the level of teaching in the first boarding school of the Society of the Sacred Heart at the moment of its founding. The publication was created in response to the request of families, as indicated by a note found on the last page: "One might have eliminated from this Program a few topics that time did not allow us to teach the Students; but in order to accommodate the desires of parents who wanted to know in detail the Plan of Studies of this house, we did not feel entitled to omit them." The names of the outstanding students were published in the *Exercises* of the end of the year. The ecclesiastics attached to the school and a few notables from the town were invited to attend.

Sophie Barat, director of the Amiens school, 1802-1804, must have contributed to the preparation of this program, in particular the program of the upper classes. Henriette Grosier, who was in charge of the intermediate classes, would have contributed as well. If one judges by the list of students appearing at the Exercises of 1805, the course of studies was implemented from 1801 to 1805. However, after 1804, Catherine de Charbonnel[21] fulfilled the role of mistress of studies as well as that of mistress general of the boarding school. The publication of this document therefore might well have been entrusted to her because she surely had the aptitude for such a project. Her biography relates the following:

---

21 Catherine-Emilie de Charbonnel de Jussac was born in 1774 in Monistrol, Haute-Loire. Her family suffered greatly during the French Revolution: her father was exiled, her brother shot.

She wrote, with incredible rigor, clear and methodical manuscripts that were designed to explain the overly brief work of Reverend Father Loriquet. She composed a geography in which she included interesting data on religions and languages, then, an extremely expansive grammar, and a practical arithmetic, judged a masterpiece by an experienced teacher who gave lessons to the younger teachers. Somewhat later, she included arithmetical charts, in which decimals and metrical calculation were explained in precise detail.[22]

Was it perhaps on the basis of this first course of geography, which brought in some aspects of astronomy, that these six students were examined during the Exercises?

At the convent of Monistrol, where her aunt was superior, Catherine had received good literary training and acquired competency in the domestic arts, but it does not seem that she would have been introduced to the study of physics. Rather, this is attributable to Cecile de Cassini. During her novitiate, 1803-1804, the great-great granddaughter of the celebrated physicist[23] would have been able to contribute to the creation of the program, as this excerpt from the Journal of the Novitiate of Paris suggests:

---

22 *Notice de la Révérende Mère de Charbonnel, Assistante et Économe Générale de la Société du Sacré-Cœur de Jésus*, par M. Dufour, Rome, A. S-C. F., p. 66.

23 Tr. note: Cecile's great-great-grandfather was Giovanni Domenico Cassini, who was invited from Italy by Louis XIV to help to set up the Paris Observatory in 1669. He is credited with discovering the rings around Saturn. Her father was an astronomer as well as a geographer. Cecile was born and raised at the observatory.

"One day when I was in the process of organizing the studies," recounted Mother Barat, "I proposed that Mlle Cecile de Cassini be put in charge of a class. She protested. 'I!' she said. 'Might I at the very least be allowed to give a few lessons on astronomy or geography? Those are the elements with which I was raised; and I am interested only in those subjects.'"

Note that before the French Revolution, Jean-Dominique de Cassini had been director of the Paris Observatory. He had also worked on the division of France into its various *départements* or counties. His new representation of France as a hexagon became part of the study of geography. With the aid of her father, Cecile was able to formulate the outlines of the program and the problems to be solved.

Nevertheless, Jean-Nicolas Loriquet could equally well have collaborated. While a very young man, he was passionate about studying the stars. And it was after his arrival in Amiens, in September, 1802, that astronomical geography became part of the program of the school run by the Fathers of the Faith. There, it replaced, in the second class, physical and political geography, which were moved into the sixth and seventh classes. While the astronomical theory was somewhat condensed, it was in keeping with the level of learning for young girls.

This program thus represents the joint efforts of the first educational community of the boarding school at Amiens and of its expert on pedagogy, the prefect of studies of the *college* [secondary school]. In order to appreciate this fully, one need only compare it, class by class, to the headings of the *Plan of Study*.

Listening Carefully to the Divine Plan

As stipulated in Article II of the first chapter of the *Plan of Study*, the third topic of instruction—the diocesan catechism and the Gospel—required a special kind of study. As such, it was not part of the end-of-year Exercises. On the other hand, the program of Church History was included. With Bossuet's *History of Religion*, the boarders were introduced into the world of higher education. This work, written in the style of the seventeenth century, was composed for the French *Dauphin*; Bossuet was his tutor. He unfolded the meaning of history. To its sweeping panorama is added a synthesis. With a single glance, the reader is invited to review the past, from the creation to our own day. The pedagogical intent of the author is to demonstrate that the king is at the service of God's plan.

Bossuet is proposed as a model for consideration. Because of the power of his thinking, he is put on the same plane as Cicero. However, this summary of the history of religion suggests a different basis of wisdom: For a world and a people marked by ignorance and idolatry, the source of salvation is Jesus Christ, come to restore the covenant between God and humanity. The focus of this study is that Church's mission is to carry out this work. Such is the guiding idea of the text.

The second chief subject matter in the fourth class is French grammar. The program includes two topics in the *Plan of Study*: "definition of grammar" and "parts of speech." The lessons begin with phonics and move to the parts of speech (noun, adjective, article, verb and pronoun) as found in Latin grammar. Regarding verb conjugation, number, tense and mood are taught.

The teaching style aims to distinguish the essential from the nonessential. By the end of the fourth class, the foundations of the French language and history have been introduced. A more detailed program might now be begun in other classes, using their respective strategies: chronology, general geography, summary or analysis of specific events.

A timeline and survey of ancient history are part of the program at this academic level. Instruction begins with terminology used to calculate time, such as the era, the sundial, an epoch, a century, an age, a year, a month, a cycle, a period, etc.

This method follows Rollin, for whom "the first concern that one should bring to the study of history, in general, is to instill order and method, in order to clearly distinguish the facts, the characters, the times, the places; chronology and geography, justifiably called the two eyes of history because they bring light and counter chaos."[24]

The examination given on "bases and certainty of chronology" lends this study a quasi-scientific aspect. *The Summary of Ancient History Both Sacred and Profane* focuses only on sacred History. The principal of division into "epochs" goes back, under a different term, to that of [Rollin] the author of *Traité d'études*. A selection of major events from the seven historical epochs is studied, disclosing new issues. In this case, the educational objective is to develop critical thinking and a love of truth. In literature, the choice of the play *Esther* is equally in line with the pedagogy supported by Rollin, with reference to Fénelon.

---

24 Rollin, *Traité des Etudes*, Volume II, *De l'histoire*, Librairie Firmin-Didot, Paris, 1877, p. 239. He distinguishes here three ways of studying history: synopsis analysis, and summary. It was after having been rector of the University of Paris that Charles Rollin (1661-1741) wrote this four-volume *Treatise on Studies* (1726-1737).

The meaning of our Redemption by Christ having been studied by the fifth and fourth classes, some play writing is appropriate. The accounts of certain events, such as "the flood and the laws of nature," "the captivity in Egypt," "the wandering in the desert," or "the Babylonian captivity," can be explained. Rollin demonstrates how idolatry and its corollary, imprisonment, are overcome by the divine initiatives expressed through these headings: the Covenant, the Coming of Christ, the Gift of the Holy Spirit to the Church on Pentecost. The theological references, seen in such expressions as "spiritual and natural Jews" or "the vocation of the Gentiles," are Pauline. The central paradigm is that of the divine Covenant.

Judged ready to graduate from stories to reasoning, the students of the third class also receive instruction in dogma. This theological initiation introduces a model of classification that will endure until 1960, the scheme of which follows:

what one must believe >	the Creed
what one must do >	the Commandments of God and the Church
what helps one to do it >	Grace and the Sacraments

The study of French grammar follows a similar sequence. After a review of the different parts of speech, it moves to "the enumeration of verbs and adverbs" and "the explanation of tenses and moods of verbs". Instruction in arithmetic, for that time, is described using first these concepts listed in the program: "What is arithmetic. – Fundamental principle of the value of numbers and of all arithmetic. – First principles of numeration." Learning engages not only empirical processes, but also the intelligence through the study of definitions and principles. At this stage, the distinctions among the Arabic, Roman and Chinese systems of numbering are given. A young student must learn the first arithmetical operations: simple addition and subtraction.

The lesson returns repeatedly to examples; whatever the level or subject matter, practice exercises allow the teacher to evaluate the student's mastery of the material. For example, in political geography, students must create a map in order to memorize facts and places. Such an exercise invokes intelligence and imagination, perception and memory. When these abilities come together, students can learn new ideas.

This teaching method supports openness to contemporary ideas. The arithmetic program includes the new metric system adopted by the Convention. The history program takes into account the dawn of a new scientific awareness, at the moment of transition between two centuries.

A Well-planned Course of Studies

From the "summary" in the fourth class and the program of "religion" in third class, students move on in the second class[25] to the study of "the history of the people of God." While covering the same historical periods, the narrative deals with major events, but far more precise attention is accorded the major figures. The recommended method is that of the summary; influenced by the Plan of Study, it adapts Charles Rollin's didactic recommendations for the education of girls. The chronology integrates "modern" history, which spans Jesus Christ to Napoleon Bonaparte. The organizing principle is that

---

25 As is the case in the third class, the author of the manual used is not named. His identity, however, is Jean-Nicolas Loriquet.

of the ascendancy of Christian civilization. It connotes a royalist ideology of restoration. Curiously, the French Revolution is skipped over, the final topic being that of the peace rendered the Church by the Concordat.

The study of the "French Language" now replaces that of grammar. This change of name marks the beginning of a reasoned analysis of speech. In literature, the program opens with the study of taste, a notion that became fashionable with Voltaire and Diderot, who distinguished taste from genius, understood as creative power. It then takes up the various literary genres: epistolary, historical, poetic and oratory. Only the first two genres are the subjects of study.

In setting out the ideas for the class in mythology, certain similarities with Christianity may be distinguished—without, however, falling into the syncretism that was then in vogue but putting the Gospel in perspective. In presenting the irrationality and senselessness of the idolatry in Greco-Roman civilization, it throws into relief the liberation arising from the coming of Jesus Christ and thereby underscores the importance given to religious formation. Instruction in the program of the second class has aspects of a class in the Humanities. This curriculum, furthermore, is unmistakably present in the subsequent class, with its study of poetry, oratory, and astronomical geography.

The history of the Church takes up again, in a more sophisticated manner, the concepts of chronology taught in the second class. The teaching of grammar is replaced by rhetoric. Metrical calculation now targets bookkeeping, the "book of accounts," which at this time takes the form of a "General Ledger" for commercial balance sheets or that of a family "Journal," also called the "Commonplace Book," in which expenditures, recipes, and family events are recounted from day to day.

"Physical and Political Geography" is a course on general culture, which today would be called an introduction to the social sciences and to moral and political philosophy. It includes the following concepts: "Summary of the history of Empires, Kingdoms, Republics in different parts of the world. – Their geographical division. – Their ancient and modern names. – Area. – Location. – Boundaries. – Climate. – Soil. – Mountains. – Forests. – Lakes. – Rivers. – Religions. – Governments. – Rulers. – Languages. – Arts and sciences. – Great men of each country. – Universities. – Population. – Income. – Ground and sea forces. – Manners and customs. – Antiquity. – Navigation. – Commerce. – Manufacturing, etc."

The study of geography is not limited to strict description, suggesting a historical purpose. It also integrates ideas that were part of the study of philosophy for young people during the eighteenth century. The following question might be seen as its synthesis and final outcome: "Might there be a reason to think about the place our earth occupies among the planets, the arrangement of its parts, and the place that we ourselves occupy within it?" With this invitation, the theoretical formulation of the course of studies draws to its close.

Within the context of a culture in which astronomical discoveries were provoking considerable curiosity and interest, the study of cosmology was considered a preferred pedagogical means by which students could ask themselves questions about the wisdom at work in the universe. Other realms of knowledge—arithmetic, geography, and history—also took on a scientific aspect. Major technological advances were on the horizon. Open to these new representations of knowledge, Sophie Barat and Jean-Nicolas Loriquet included them in the program.

The realm of humanistic training has two defining reference points: sacred history and cosmology.[26] As noted earlier, one vision of the world is developed through study of the *Abridged History of Religion*. Its first concept is that of the creation of the world and of the human being. In the final analysis, this resonates with the question posed regarding the *reason* for human existence and the cosmos. Its inclusion is significant. From the outset, a worldwide drama is proposed at the beginning and then expanded throughout the last four years of the educational curriculum. At its end, the student is invited to participate with discernment.

Along the way, the concepts taught aim to prepare the young minds for this kind of thinking. Translated in terms of educational objectives, they offer direction trajectory:

- to know how to read and write;
- to know the history of the people of God;
- to be capable of administering a household and, among other things, to maintain household accounts;
- to know one's cultural roots and the characteristics of other civilizations and religions;
- to discover the meaning of life and communicate it to others.

---

26 The discovery of the planet Uranus in the eighteenth century, followed by that of Pluto in the nineteenth, led to the study of the different constellations within the galaxy.

Their first readings in sacred history have familiarized them with what is at issue. The forms of idolatry in ancient Greece, leading to a rupture of the Covenant with the Creator and Savior, are considered in studying mythology. Exemplary figures of courage, integrity, and faithfulness have been studied in literature and sacred Scripture. These pedagogical references define an area in which the various human faculties—sensibility, imagination, intelligence, and memory—are called upon one by one in the act of learning, resulting in a fully realized education for young women.

At the end of the course of study, the educator must complete one last task: to propose a personal synthesis, an indispensable stage of reflection before elaborating the project of a personal, well-ordered life. This is the goal of the final class.

This additional course features two principal axes: a synthesis of the coursework and the study of rhetoric. Set beside astronomical geography, this teaching satisfies the educational goal to which the new Institute is committed. Because in order to glorify the Heart of Christ, it is not enough to discover the design of God in the workings of the universe—it must be communicated to others, to the largest number possible, and beyond the frontiers. Only in this way would the *original idea of the little Society* be realized. The aptitude of the young women to communicate intelligently a way of life is demonstrated in the *Provisional Plan of Study*, written in 1804.

However, if this training, intended at first for men, suggests intellectual competencies of the highest order, it does not for all that destroy the predominantly feminine quality of the educational climate at the Amiens House. Two notebooks of songs from this early period point this out. These verses help spread values by an effective means: music and songs. They also demonstrate how the educational goals are expressed in terms of educative interaction and moral development. The virtues of courage, faithfulness and gratitude; the feeling for competition; and the joy of victory, kindness, and filial trust are especially highlighted.[27]

If the pedagogical design can be partially traced to that of Rollin, the criteria for progressing from one class to the next is clearly influenced by the division of humanities[28] classes according to the rules of grammar found in the Jesuit *Ratio Studiorum*. "Five classes lead the student from the basics to the threshold of philosophy, according to their well-tailored and precisely adjusted levels; as the grades advance, the classes in grammar, the humanities, and rhetoric follow three levels of concepts: enumeration, description, interpretation." This course matches that of the *Provisional Plan of Study used in the house of Amiens*. Nevertheless, in order to maintain that the educational model is that of the Jesuits, a final element remains to be verified: the teaching method.

"In a Way That Is Familiar to Us"

In 1805, Cardinal Fesch called Jean-Nicolas Loriquet to

---

27   Some of these poems were written by J.-N. Loriquet: "His easygoing Muse not only interpreted the feelings of the students at the *Oratoire*, but readily lent itself in 1803 to express the wishes and the gratitude of the young girls in this Christian house of instruction to their superior," A. Guidée, *Vie du Révérend Père Loriquet*, idem, p. 72.

28   "The Jesuits, beginning with Ignatius, attached enormous importance to these stages of learning; they believed that to establish a course of rhetoric wherein students had not already been prepared by the humanities would be a complete waste of time: it would be, they said, a house built upon the sand." F. de Dainville, p. 85.

Argentière, near Lyon, to open a *collège*-seminary. There he wrote a plan of studies[29] whose "preliminary observations" mention the educational traditions to which he is referring[30]: "Fleury, Jouvency, Pluche, Rollin, those are the men whom I have consulted and from whom I have gathered my principles. But it is Jouvency who has been our principal guide, and in many places, our plan is nothing more than the development of that which he traced in his first work entitled *Discendi et Docendi*."

If the "principal guide" is Jouvency, the method of teaching references the *Ratio Studiorum* of the Society of Jesus.[31] In fact, at the *collège* of Argentière, the class exercises are scheduled:

a – First half-hour: recitation of lessons;
b – Second and third half hours: explication of Latin writers;
c – Fourth half-hour: correction of homework;
d – Fifth half-hour: assignment of homework.

This distribution of the scholarly schedule, morning and evening, can be found in chapter III of the *Plan of Study* for the young women. The parameters found in the introduction—allocation of time wisely managed, order of lessons and teaching

---

29 The course of studies extends across ten classes, from the eighth class to the study of philosophy. *Plan d'Études pour le Collège-Séminaire de l'Argentière,* Arch. Prov. Camp. E.F.140a.

30 In fact, no precursor can be said to be at the origins of a particular educational institution or system. Education, insofar as it is an institution, always precedes us; by the same token, no human being is at the origins of language. F. Marty, *La bénédiction de Babel,* chap. I, Cerf, 1990, p. 21, sq.

31 *Ratio Studiorum, Plan raisonné et institution des études dans la Compagnie de Jésus,* édition bilingue latin-français présentée par M-M. Compère, Belin, 1997.

method—work together. Whatever the level (or grade), the sequence of lessons is the same:

Fifteen minutes for spelling is inserted in the morning, between reading and the correction of homework.

10-15 minutes	Recitation of lessons
10-15 minutes	Reading
10-15 minutes	Correction of homework
30 minutes	Explanation: [Oral lesson] Assignment of homework

Another aspect of this "allocation of time wisely managed" is the time of day at which these classes are situated: 9 o'clock in the morning, 3 o'clock in the afternoon. They last a fairly short time: an hour and a half in the morning, an hour in the afternoon. Each class is preceded by a half hour of study. In the morning, it is followed by an hour of writing; in the afternoon, by two hours of manual work.

A problem-solving method engages by turns the imagination, the memory, and the intelligence. In designing a geographical map, in putting together a book of accounts, or in composing a poem, students learn to master rules. The new intellectual skill becomes an interpersonal skill, an essential aspect of the teaching of culture. In integrating into oneself a new cultural fact or figure, the person finds herself transformed, enriched. In the best-case scenario, she is also capable of communicating and transmitting to others what she herself has received. This is clearly the aim of Jesuit pedagogy.

The student's degree of comprehension and advancement is at the center of this methodology. The "cardinal rule"—"one thing at a time, step by step, to each according to her abilities,"³²—determines the didactic choices.

This metaphor of "drop by drop" is recommended for the instruction of boarding students: "When one speaks to the children, one must limit the amount of knowledge one attempts to impart because there are limits to what they can absorb. It is above all important not to introduce too many things at once: it is essential, so to speak, to introduce ideas into their minds one by one, as one introduces a liquid drop by drop into a vase whose opening is narrow: if you pour in too much all at once, the liquid goes everywhere, and nothing goes into the vase."³³

This method underlies the conception of *The Provisional Plan of Study Used in the House of Amiens*. The sequence applies to the daily schedule, the program, and the teaching style. Assigning a grade, or the condition for admission into a class, divides the course of studies into as many levels as are needed to meet the goal: to think for oneself. The lessons, arranged within a schedule, are also arranged with respect to one another "in a manner that is familiar to us"³⁴: recitation of lessons, correction of homework, explication of selected passages, and practical exercises.

These three elements, characteristic of the approach, might be schematized as follows:

---

32 Codina Mir, *Aux sources de la pédagogie des Jésuites, Le "modus parisiensis"* Institutum historicum, Rome, p. 106.

33 Lhomond, *Éléments de la grammaire française, revus et augmentés par J-N. Loriquet*, Préface de l'auteur, Rusand, Lyon, 1818, A. FSJ., E F 266, p. X.

34 This expression is used by F. de Dainville, in the work cited above, in order to describe the teaching method of the University of Paris, taken up by the first companions of Ignatius of Loyola.

ORDER	
Teaching Method	Time
Goal of instruction	

The opening of *The Provisional Plan of Study Used in the House of Amiens* explains it in these terms: "The success of a Plan of Study essentially depends on the allocation of time wisely managed, on the order of lessons, and on the teaching method."

"Appropriate for Young Ladies"

There are significant differences in the content of literature classes. There is scarcely a book list. All that is specified is:
- for each class: the diocesan catechism and the Gospel, French grammar, the Fables of La Fontaine.
- in third class, *Esther*;
- in second class, *Athalie*;
- in first class, the *Poème de la Religion*, the *Christian Doctrine of Man,* and *The Lessons of Nature* by Cousin Despreaux;
- in superior class, *The Foundations of Faith* and *The Lessons of Nature.*

As to the teaching of French language and literature, it was limited to that which was "appropriate for young ladies." The levels are,[35] from lowest to highest:

Lower classes: fourth class; third class.

Higher classes: second class, first class, superior class.

---

35 This division corresponds to that of all high schools at the beginning of the nineteenth century. O Gréart, *Éducation et Instruction,* tome II, Paris, Hachette, 1887, Annexe #1, p. 246-247.

In the fourth class, the program of French grammar corresponds to that of the lower class of grammar at the young men's college. In the third, it coincides in part with the middle level of grammar. But it also introduces literature through the study of the epistolary genre, which is begun only in the humanities class at Argentière.

In the second class, the level of the grammar is equivalent to that of the middle class; in first, to that of the advanced grammar class. However, the literature program of the second and first classes at the Amiens school seems to correspond to that of the humanities class at the *collège* of Argentière. Both history and poetry are studied there; and oratory is begun. The Fables of La Fontaine correspond, in terms of the overall course of studies, to those of the lower grammar classes for the boys. The first books (*Aesop's Fables and Phèdre,* translated verse) are very short and meant especially for children.

Nevertheless, in the literature program for the first class, classical literature is taught together with Greco-Roman culture, and classical authors through translations. Some examples are:

- pastoral poetry: Theocritus, Moschus, Bion, Virgil;
- lyric poetry: Pindar, Anacreon, Horace;
- dramatic poetry: Aeschylus, Sophocles, Euripides,
- epic poetry: Homer, Virgil, Lucan, Cavallo, Alamani, etc.

And in the superior class, the study of rhetoric adopts several works from the program at the college of Argentière: *On Oratorical Invention, On the Oratorical Disposition, On*

Oratorical Elocution. On Action.[36]

The curse of studies at the Amiens boarding school is coordinated with the Humanities, following a choice expressed by Ignatius Loyola. "Literature, which prepares one for everything and provides for everything, is the best means for training the Latin orator and enabling him to master the 'eternal and divine' word, which seems as indispensable to the theologian as to him whom one will later call an honest man."[37] As is the case at the *collège*-seminary of Argentière, the organizing principle of the plan of studies for the young women is graded access to classical literature. But it is not the study of Latin grammar that characterizes the "degrees" that lead to rhetoric. The French language is both "the essential objective of teaching and of the dividing line between classes." How do we interpret this choice? Is it a sign of modernity or an accommodation to cultural prejudices?

Both motives must have come into play, and it is difficult for us to estimate which of the two might have prevailed. The choice of the vernacular language as the basis for learning is expressed, from Jean-Baptiste de la Salle to Condorcet, in this historical order:

- 17th century: J.B. de la Salle – Comenius – Oratorians – Port Royal
- Fleury, *Traité du choix et de la méthode des* études;
- 18th century: Rollin, *Traité des Etudes* – The Encyclopedists – La Chalotais, *Essai d'éducation nationale*;

---

36 J.-N. Loriquet, *Plan d'Études du Collège-Séminaire de l'Argentière*, Article de la Rhétorique, p. 31.
37 F. de Dainville, p. 24.

Condorcet and the plans of study at the time of the Constitutional Assembly.

For all of these pedagogues, "learning Latin before learning one's mother tongue was wanting to ride horseback before knowing how to walk." Previously, students had been introduced to reading through Latin, even in the primary schools. This permitted students to follow the religious services and to receive a solid religious training, deemed necessary at the time of the Counter-Reformation. Jean-Baptiste de la Salle began to break with this educational tradition. Concerned with adapting education to the social conditions of poor children, in the face of the need for brief schooling before a lifetime of work, he opted for the mother tongue.[38] Following this, Rollin also recommended the study of principles in the vernacular language for a diverse student population. Condorcet moved the study of Latin to the college level. The choice of the literature program in the *Plan of Study* of 1804 was part of this trend.

Nevertheless, in this adaptation to modernity, the constraints of social prejudice cannot be underestimated. In fact, according to Rollin, women "are in no way destined to instruct people, govern Nations, wage war, render justice, plead causes, or practice medicine. Their place is within the home, and limits itself to functions that are not less useful, but less laborious and more in line with the mildness of their character, the delicacy

---

38 Yves Poutet, *Genèse et caractéristiques de la pédagogie lasallienne*, Ed. Don Bosco, Collection "Sciences de l'éducation" dirigée par Guy Avanzini, Paris, 1995, p. 169-70.

of their complexion, and their natural inclinations."[39] And in the nineteenth century, this idea still determined the teaching of girls: "To the extent that scholarly manuals are available to them, the content must be summarized in a manner that suits the young ladies."[40]

Such discrimination would persist for a long while. The following regulation, proclaimed on March 7, 1837, for the Female Institutions of the Department of the Seine, was recognized as law: "The tradition is there, so restrictive that it seems to go without saying: girls should have access neither to Latin, nor to the study of philosophy, which is judged to be dangerous for their modesty and for the development of their minds."[41] The true openness to modernity within the 1804 Plan of Study was to have chosen to include an introduction to rhetoric and cosmology. Such a decision represented a break with the thinking of the time.

It took only four years to establish the educational foundations of the fledgling Institute. The speed with which these programs had been put in place was made possible by the support of Jean-Nicolas Loriquet and the choice of an Ignatian educational model. The *Ratio studiorum*'s method was adapted to the Institute's own goal: to know the limitless love of Christ and to make it known to others. Such was, indeed, the underlying goal of the original educational plan. It arises from the Thomist notion of the human person whose first perfection is to know

---

39 C. Rollin, *Traité des Etudes*, Tome I, Livre premier, chapitre II, De l'éducation des filles, p. 75.

40 F. Mayeur, *L'Éducation des filles au XIXe siècle*, Hachette, Paris, 1979, p. 8.

41 *Histoire mondiale de l'éducation,* chapitre III, Origines, utopies et principes, La ségrégation des filles, p. 135.

God and the second, to act in a way that reflects divine *agape*.

The study of the *Provisional Plan of Study in Use at the House of Amiens* and its program makes clear an overall direction, moving from elementary studies to rhetoric and physics. The goal of the educational plan is to form judgment—to develop intelligence and critical thinking—in a way that catalyzes one's own discovery of the meaning of life and of the universe.

At the beginning of the nineteenth century, it was truly audacious to develop a curriculum all the way through to the study of rhetoric. It marked a major step forward in the instruction of young girls. Women were deemed capable of contributing, through their judgment and their influence, to the reconstruction of the social fabric based on Christian values. But in the wake of the French Revolution, would this conviction promote an alternate image of women and their social status? Would the original idea be thwarted or maintained?

CHAPTER II

Adoption of the Initial Plan

VERY QUICKLY, A SERIES OF TRIALS IMPOSED by the Ministry prevented Joseph Varin from exercising his role as superior general. By decree of the Messidor (June 22, 1804), the Fathers of the Faith were dissolved because their secondary schools were overshadowing the reputation of the state schools. And in 1806, constrained to leave the Collège de Saint-Acheul near Amiens, the Fathers moved to Montdidier. A year later, they were ordered to practice their ministry in their home parishes.

At his own instigation, Sambucy de Saint-Estève was incardinated in the diocese of Amiens, and it was at this moment that he assumed control of the establishment of the Ladies of Christian Instruction. The political climate being favorable, he profited from the superior general's departure for his family home and took his place. At this point, he drew up a Plan of Education, but it was rewritten in 1810. What prompted it? And did it relate to the original plan?

II.1 A Fomenter of Discord

When Winds of Division Blow
After the departure of Mme Barat to take over the boarding school of Sainte-Marie-d'En-Haut in Grenoble, responsibilities within the Amiens boarding school were reorganized. The Annual Report for the year 1806 lists the following duties:
>Mesdames A. Baudemont, Director
>C. de Charbonnel, Mistress General of Classes
>Ad. Bardot, Mistress of the First Class
>M. du Terrail, Mistress of the Second Class
>M. Olivier, Mistress of the Third Class
>M. Ducis, Mistress of the Fourth Class.

Beginning in 1806, under the joint leadership of Mme Baudemont[42] and the Abbé Sambucy de Saint-Estève, disagreements developed among the members of the new Institute. The dispute centered on both the Ignatian model of a centralized government and the school's pedagogical identity. When the first General Assembly gathered in Amiens on January 18, 1806, Sophie Barat was confirmed superior general for life; she received only one vote more than Anne Baudemont. Several months later, the determination to replace her reappeared in the Amiens boarding school's application for legal approval.

---

42 Anne Baudemont had negotiated with M. de Saint-Genis, President of the Criminal Tribunal, the escape of J.-N. Loriquet from the prison of Reims on August 15, 1797. This fact brought her a level of respect, acknowledgment and esteem on the part of the Fathers of the Faith. One can thus understand why Joseph Varin would have admitted this former Poor Clare into the new Institute and conferred on her the directorship of the boarding school in 1804. See A. Guidée, *Vie du Révérend Père Loriquet, de la Compagnie de Jésus,* Poussielgue-Rusand, Paris, 1845, A. S-C.F., p. 45.

This move took aim at the stability of the new Institute. And it took place within a critical national context. Between 1800 and 1803, other teaching or nursing congregations had obtained government authorization to operate. However, oddly, the application submitted to the Ministry was not made in the name of Mme Barat, but in that of Mme Baudemont. Nevertheless, the official statute's second and third articles clearly stipulate the newness of the legal procedures of the congregation. They distinguish its functions quite clearly:

Article 2

Their Company is governed by a superior general, elected by the majority of members and assisted by a council named by the same majority.

Article 3

The nomination of local superiors, the assignment and reassignment of the members, is at the discretion of the superior general.[43]

Furthermore, at the beginning of March 1807, Father Varin let Mme Barat know that Monsignor Jauffret had submitted the request for approval and the statutes of the association to the Emperor, through the intermediary of Portalis, the Minister of Religion. A temporary decree of approval from the Secretary of State was signed on March 10, 1807. It duly documents the new form of religious life.[44] In April, during a stay in Paris, the

---

43   Statutes of the Ladies of Christian Instruction, A.G.S-C.-IV, p.1.

44   "The Association of the Ladies of Christian Instruction may admit new members, as long as they conform to the laws of the Empire, which prohibits perpetual vows." Napoleon, Emperor of France and King of Italy, Excerpt from the Minutes of the Secretary of State, at the Imperial Camp of Osterode, March 10, 1807, Art. IV., A.G.S-C, p. 1.

superior general received word of the legal authorization. And in May 1807, Minister Portalis sent the decree to the Prefect of the Somme, Quinette, and to the bishop of Amiens, Bishop Demandolx. On May 24, 1807, he communicated the news to Mme Baudemont, who immediately spread the word to the notables of the city, the ecclesiastics, the religious houses, and to the benefactors of the establishment, including the mother of the Emperor. In response, congratulatory letters went to the Abbé de Saint-Estève or to Mme Baudemont. None of them made mention of the superior general. For the local civil authorities and some students' parents, the title of superior seemed to refer to Mme Baudemont.

The legal approval accorded by the Emperor gave the directors of the Amiens school a certain panache and contributed to the recruitment of students. Thus, by October 5, 1807, the number of boarding students had reached sixty-six; the number of students in the free school remained at one hundred fifty. The community was expanding. Encouraged by Sambucy de Saint-Estève, Anne Baudemont began to admit former nuns, driven out of their convents during the Revolution. The religious model of the House of Amiens, which was meant to function as the motherhouse, shifted to that of earlier self-governing convents.

Father Varin did not seem to be aware of this new direction. He allowed the Abbé de Saint-Estève, who was doing all in his power to rewrite the text of the Constitutions of the new Institute according to the model of the Ursulines and the Visitation nuns, to function in his name. At the same time, the usurper attempted to suppress the educational plan put in place between

1801 and 1805. In 1806, he wrote a new educational plan and assumed for himself the leadership of the boarding school.

The Educational Plan of 1806

A notable change came to the Amiens House of Christian Education beginning in 1805. The end-of-year exercises took on a worldly guise. This penchant for showiness can be directly attributed to the Abbé Sambucy de Saint-Estève. However, the splendor of the ceremony at the graduation exercises of 1805 and the publication of the program unleashed bitter criticism. A report of it follows:

> An article published in an Italian newspaper was immediately reprinted in the French papers. One read about a society of *femmes savantes*,[45] which had just been established. Animated by the spirit of both Saint Francis de Sales and Fénelon, they were consecrated as *Dilette di Gesù*, etc. People in society were talking about it in various ways: some joked, particularly on account of the notion of *femmes savantes* and the predictions made about a forthcoming new order and the positive impact it would have on society as a whole. Others, though fewer, blessed God and exalted his mercy in view of what they saw as a means adapted to the needs of the century and destined to lay the groundwork, in the long run, for the social regeneration they hoped for with all their hearts.[46]

---

45 Tr. Note: Best translated as *bluestocking* in English; literally, *women scholars* or *learned women*.

46 Joséphine de Coriolis, *Histoire de la Société du Sacré-Cœur de Jésus*. Cited by Phil Kilroy, *Madeleine-Sophie Barat, A Life,* Cork University Press, Cork, Ireland, 2000, p. 198.

These conflicting reactions had their effect. One must ask whether the 1806 plan of education had as its ultimate goal the silencing of potential critics.

In fact, the document was submitted to the Mayor of Amiens. The statistical and administrative yearbook for the Department of the Somme for the year 1806 relays this favorable opinion: "The city of Amiens boasts four boarding schools for young ladies. We place at the head of the list that of Madame Baudemont, known by the name Boarding School of the Ladies of the Institute of Amiens." The wholesomeness and spaciousness of the school are highlighted.[47] The educational goal of the institute reads "domestic utility," an objective that will determine the structure and the pedagogical choices of the educational plan. Rhetoric and astronomy are stricken from the program. But most notably, none of the guiding principles of the provisional plan are to be found. The plan implies a distrust of the larger world. Instead, the traditional "feminine" virtues of submission, gentleness, and self-effacement are praised. The models are Fleury, Fénelon, and Mme de Maintenon, pedagogues from whom "girls should seek out only those elements of knowledge that will be useful in their future role as mothers."[48]

This return to the ideals of the eighteenth century might well have had as its objective the reassuring of the girls' parents, nervous about their daughters' becoming *femmes savantes*. But it might equally have been intended to obtain the legal approval

---

[47] Extract from the statistical and administrative directory for the Department of the Somme in the year 1806. A.G.S-C, D-I, I-a.

[48] J. de Viguerie, *Histoire mondiale de l'éducation*, Vol. I, Le mouvement des idées pédagogiques aux XVIIe et XVIIIe siècles, published under the direction of G. Mialaret et J. Vial, P.U.F., 1981, p. 285.

of the boarding school at Amiens, because "domestic utility" was the educational purpose also chosen by Napoleon for his newly established Legion of Honor boarding schools for girls. In the planning stage for the boarding school in Ecouen, the Emperor specified that a teacher's ultimate goal was "to form believers and not reasoners."[49] In order to justify this choice, he resorts to a backward-looking idea: "The weakness of women's brains, the instability of their ideas, their destiny within the social order, the requirement for an endless compliance, and a kind of considerate and easygoing charity: all of this can only be developed through Religion—through a religion that is charitable and meek." As a result, all instruction was merely rudimentary. The study of foreign languages was prohibited, as were rhetoric and astronomy. Rivalry and competition had no rightful place. Destiny confined the young ladies of Ecouen to the pantry, to sewing, and to the medicine chest.

In writing the Plan of Education of 1806, the Abbé de Saint Estève therefore may have had in mind two goals: the reputation of the Amiens boarding school and its legal approval. In any case, the prescriptive nature of the plan did not last. Another document replaced it four years later.

The Plan of Studies of 1810

Since 1804, Catherine de Charbonnel had been mistress general of the Amiens boarding school. In 1810, she was sent to Poitiers. Before her departure, she must have written this document with reference to the provisional plan, because the two

---

49 R. Rogers, *Les démoiselles de la Légion d'honneur,* Appendix I, Lettre de Finkenstein written by Napoleon 1st to M. de Lacépède, Grand Chancellor of the Legion of Honor, May 15, 1806, Plon, 1992, p. 332-335.

plans share a fundamental design. A key element of the 1804 plan is taken up by that of 1810: the recurrence of a division of the course of studies into five classes. And the organizing principles of the course of studies of 1804 are equally clear. On the other hand, changes are apparent in the document's orientation, the value accorded some subjects, and the level of instruction. The section on learning includes new subjects (handwriting, religion, the *arts d'agrément*—dancing, drawing, and music) as well as instructional exercises (repetitions and compositions). The list of books and manuals points to a range of human culture broader than that of the original humanities. Chronology, history, and mythology are its core elements. The study of history has become a prerequisite in the education of girls;[50] it teaches them how to put political events into perspective and contributes to the shaping of character, in the same way that Greco-Roman models function for linguists.

In terms of learning methods, the most often applied intellectual activity is memorization, at the expense of reflection and forward thinking. And above all, a perceptible drop in the academic level is apparent from the earliest classes. In the fourth class, there is no arithmetic. There is no study of the *Fables of La Fontaine*. The pruning back intensifies in the third class. Eliminated subjects include: ecclesiastical history; Roman history; geography; in literature, the epistolary genre, *Esther*, and the *Fables of La Fontaine*; and in arithmetic, decimal and metrical calculation, fractions, and advanced word problems. Instead, a study of the "Little Catechism of Fleury" is

---

50 C. Rollin, *Traité des études*, Vol. I, Chap. II, Librairie de Firmin-Didot, Paris, 1877, p. 82.

introduced. The teaching of the "lower classes" descends to an extremely elementary level, centered on the study of religion through memorization.

In the "upper classes" the cuts to the program are obvious. The standard for the humanities classes has practically disappeared; the superior class is no longer an introductory class for the study of rhetoric and theology.

In second class, history is no longer taught. Church history and the history of France are moved into the first class. The works of Racine—*Athalie* and *Esther*—reappear. Added to these are the works of Boileau.

In the first class the study of poetry has been eliminated. In its place is a course on *Christian Doctrine* by Lhomond. Note, too, that concepts in arithmetic, taught in the third class in the Provisional Plan of 1840, are deferred until this year. Bookkeeping focuses on calculations of interest, change, value of coinage, and measurements.

The superior class loses the very things that characterized it: the introduction to theology, the study of rhetoric, and natural history. It is reduced instead to a "review of what has been studied in the other classes."

The initial vision has thus been left behind. The chosen subjects are no longer in sync with the original goal: to prepare young minds to recognize the action of the Creator at work in the history of humanity. The specific character of the Provisional Plan of 1804 has been erased. The reactionary current of the Amiens school has resulted in a return to the educational style of the convents of the Ancien Régime, featuring a different representation of women and their social role. It is, moreover, part of a national, post-revolutionary movement. A set of rules, added to the plan of studies, offers further proof of this. These directives take on the appearance of a *Ratio*, which curiously evokes the *Customs and Traditions of the Paris of 1705 in the Order of Saint Ursula*. Did the educational model of Monistrol[51] perhaps serve as a guideline?

Rules in Use within the Educational Community

The document consists of two parts. The first presents the "Rules for the mistress general of classes." The second puts forward "shared and specific rules" of the mistresses of classes and the surveillantes[52] and ends with several models of manuals and meetings for the boarding school.

A summary of the first part follows:

Rules of the Mistress General of Classes
1. Concerning students in general
2. Comings and goings of students
3. Religious exercises
4. Classes
5. Discipline
6. Student ribbons of merit
7. Students who are ill

Relations of the mistress general with various persons
1. with the superior
2. with the assistant
3. with the treasurer

---

51 Tr. Note: Monistrol sur Loire was the location of the Ursuline convent founded in 1634.

52 Tr. Note: the term *surveillante* indicates a religious who is charged with school discipline and student behavior.

4. with the mistress of choir
5. with the mistress of chant
6. with the sacristan
7. with the first mistresses
8. with the surveillantes
9. with the mistress of sewing
10. with the wardrobe mistress
11. with the mistress of health and the infirmary
12. with the mistress of pharmacy
13. with the coadjutrix sisters[53] attached to the boarding school

The subdivision is significant. Seven articles have to do with classes and teaching; thirteen involve relations with other members of the educational community. Running the organization is the responsibility of the mistress general, in concert with the local superior and the other educators. The list of duties indicates her central place. This role may be a legacy of the monastic schools?

The rules of 1705 for the Company of Saint Ursula accorded the mistress general[54] a privileged place. But the organizing principle of the regulations is the order to be maintained, in accordance with a wise distribution of responsibilities. In the Amiens boarding school, management is no longer centralized. The mistress general holds in her hands the cogs and wheels

---

53   Tr. Note: Coadjutrix sisters were distinguished from the teaching nuns. They would have taken religious vows, but their duties would have been to cook, clean, and otherwise serve the material needs of the house.

54   *Règlements des Ursulines de la Congrégation de Paris*, Archives de Paris, pp. 7-23.

of the entire educational institution thus reinforcing the dependency of the remaining personnel. In addition, the studies concentrate more on intellectual formation. This insistence is obvious from the earliest classes. The first schoolmistresses are asked "to make students advance as much as possible in reading and writing, giving preference even over handwork." And to the substitute teachers in these classes, it is recommended to "do everything possible to shape the reason of the students." The list of "Rules for the Mistress General of Classes" deals essentially with consultation, coordination and supervision of studies. Intellectual development is specifically mandated.[55]

This set of ideas is based therefore not that of the monastery of Saint Ursula, but on the Jesuit *Ratio Studiorum*. The prototype could perhaps have come from the Sisters of Notre Dame.

Françoise Soury-Lavergne asserts, in fact, that after 1705, rules were added to the customs of the Company of Notre-Dame—"rules that contained among other things a document organized as follows:

The Order and Establishment of the Schools of the Company of Notre-Dame:
    Rules for the Superior
    Rules for the Prefect of Classes
    Rules for the Regents
    Rules for the Schoolgirls.

The historian also makes clear that "these pages largely reproduced the moral counsels of the *Ratio Studiorum* and

---

55 However, the care for the students' food and clothing as well as their physical development recall the *Règlements des religieuses Ursulines de la congrégation de Paris*.

emphasized for the teachers a deep concern for with Christian formation."[56]

This document might well have served as a basis for the description of the organization of the educational community at the boarding school of Amiens.

The Rules of 1810 also specify that the healthy functioning of an institution requires true interdependence: "They must support one another, speaking insofar as possible the same language." The argument admits no alternative: "They are working toward the same end, and they should employ the same means." However, in 1810, this shared educational vision is not yet explicit. In fact, it will not be achieved until 1815 with the writing of the Constitutions of the Society of the Sacred Heart.

The Identity of the Founder

The reactionary strategy of the Abbé Sambucy de Saint-Estève and Anne Baudemont inevitably brought with it an institutional crisis. In 1811, the communities of Ghent, Grenoble, Poitiers, and Niort refused to accept the Constitutions written by the Abbé de Saint-Estève. In 1812, the house in Ghent, Belgium, directed by Mme de Peñaranda, separated from the French houses. At the Amiens convent, a divisive spirit reigned. Most of the members openly expressed their opposition to the superior general. And when, in 1814, the Jesuits were reinstated, the crisis became bitter.

Having discovered the aspirations of the Abbé Sambucy de Saint-Estève, Father Varin wished to help the religious of the Amiens house to rediscover their clear vision and their identity.

---

56 F. Soury-Lavergne, *Chemin d'éducation sur les traces de J. de Lestonnac, 1556-1640*, Rome, 1984, p. 328.

He came to stay for a few days and gave several conferences. The conference of June 4, 1814, was a history of the institute, organized around several themes:
    a – identity of the founder;
    b – the Ignatian design of the original plan;
    c – the social function and style of dress of the educators;
    d – professional competency and the practice of prayer;
    e – identity of the Institute;
    f – spirituality of the founder and of the two Societies;[57]
    g – identity of the audience.

Three elements are particularly significant: the identification of the founder; the setting forth of the constituent elements of the initial plan; and the identity of the audience recorded by Father de Tournély.

The identity of the founder, as expressed in "a" above, and the spirituality of the founder, as expressed in "f" above, are uncommonly alike:

a

Father Varin clarifies first that he does not regard himself as the founder (God forbid) but as the successor to Father de Tournély, from whom he drew all his insights and objectives. It is his responsibility to convey to us his thinking and his spirit and he is faithfully committed to doing so. However, he continues, what were Father de Tournély's goals?

---

57 The Fathers of the Faith would eventually become integrated into the Jesuit Order, suppressed in France in 1764 and restored in 1814.

f

What would motivate these young women? It is this: the spirit of Father de Tournély, your founder, a spirit of humility, of generosity, of obedience. There are the virtues with which he was filled and which he regarded as being at the foundation of the two Societies.

As in every origin story, in calling up the memory of the past, Joseph Varin takes aim at the heart of the intrigue. In identifying the founder, he indirectly denounces the usurper—the fomenter of trouble and division. In order to defuse the conflict, he asserts that no one can claim such a role and thereby signifies that the current difficulties in the school reveal an illegitimate appropriation of institutional power.

The second significant element of the account concerns the canonical form of the Institute Léonor de Tournély hoped for. The professional demands and the criteria for a suitable style of dress are linked to him, cleverly juxtaposed with the tastes and the intentions of the founder through expressions like "he wanted . . . , he desired . . . ." This reminder aims directly at the essential and so helps his listeners to put turmoil and conflict behind them. The third significant element, the spiritual identity of the audience, is not approached head-on but through a kind of crescendo. Once again, the narrator relates the intentions of the founder: "But what was the spirit with which he wanted these young women to be motivated? It is this: the spirit of Father de Tournély, your founder." Thus, the spirituality of the new Institute and that of the founder are associated at once by means of a question and answer format. The closing words of the account offer the final proof. In order to achieve spiritual liberty—a prerequisite for a clear conscience in belonging to the Institute—one is advised to imitate the virtues of the founder: humility, generosity, and obedience.

The institute's three chief characteristics follow. A first feature restricts the institute's mission to education. A fourth vow is linked to it. It describes the institute's apostolic orientation, guaranteeing the continuity of social action across the fluctuations of history. The second feature concerns the practice of prayer, the foundation of the educational enterprise. Its placement here confirms its necessity. The third feature underlines the spiritual identity of the educators: "to be consecrated to the Sacred Heart of Jesus, engaged in a perpetual act of adoration." To live in the presence of the risen Christ and always to call upon its strength defines the very way of being and behaving of a religious of the Institute. The source, used metaphorically, points to the central image: the open Side of Christ.

Setting forth these essential features confirms the Congregation's chief characteristics. By including the third feature, Father Varin joined the insight of Léonor de Tournély with the *original idea of the little Society* of Sophie Barat. These two might be considered co-founders. On the other hand, the immediate cause of de Tournély's insight was omitted; because any reminder of past ambiguity regarding educational plans would risk adding to the current confusion. In its place was an emphasis on cloister. The expression "truly religious and truly cloistered" confirms that one of the key points of controversy between the followers of the Abbé de Saint-Estève and the superior general concerned cloister. In fact, Saint-Estève wanted to return to the earlier notion of monasteries with autonomous governments.[58] Following that design, the centrality of the "work of Religion" prohibits flexibility of tasks or roles. Thus, any activities that would sidetrack the religious from the principal mission must be avoided; the most radical means to avoid such a thing is regulation through cloister.

That being said, accounts of the first schools indicate some openness to variety on this point. The case of Cuignières, in 1808, is conclusive on this point. This foundation responded to the possible need to relocate the Amiens school in the country not far from Amiens, because the suspicions held by Fouché[59] with respect to the association[60] of the Fathers of the Faith were beginning to affect the community of women. However, the contract signed on March 2, 1808, with the commune of Cuignières, near Beauvais, included a variety of endeavors for the religious: the education of boarding students, teaching catechism to the young villagers on Sunday mornings, visits and nursing care for sick parishioners, upkeep of the church and the sacristy.[61] The Cuignières residents made an offer through the intermediation of M. Bailly, proprietor of the school, that had in fact a double objective: to guarantee a good education for their daughters and to benefit from the nursing skills provided

---

58 See C. Langlois, *Le catholicisme au féminin, Les congrégations françaises à supérieure générale au XIXe siècle*, Cerf, 1984, p. 85.

59 Tr. Note: Joseph Fouché (1759-1820) headed Napoleon's secret police.

60 Quinette, Prefect of the Somme, compromised himself during these accusations. P. Biérot, "The Fathers of the Faith in the Diocese of Amiens," *Bulletin de la Société des Antiquaires de Picardie* (1939-40), Bibliothèque municipale d'Amiens, p. 153.

61 *Rélation, Sur la Fondation de Cuignières*, A. S-C, F, B – 05 – 117, p. 21.

by the Sisters of Charity before the Revolution. In an uncertain political environment, this fourth foundation of the Ladies of Christian Instruction took up the apostolic plan envisioned by Léonor de Tournély: a range of services in response to the needs of the local situation. This foundation might be considered atypical, given its urgent character. But isn't it through such situations that the originality of a work can be seen?

The conference held in Amiens on June 4, 1814, sheds light on how the original plan is being interpreted a few years later. If Léonor de Tournély is the founder, Father Varin is the one who brought it to its fulfillment. And in this very specific situation, Varin insists on adherence to canon law and obedience to the Church. His moral authority had to be acknowledged by the dissenting members. In reminding them of the intentions of the founder, he aims at diffusing the conflicts, at overcoming division. Such are the high stakes of this foundational document.

The message is clear. The identity of a congregation supersedes the vagaries of its development. It stems from the original plan and not from some other set of random factors. It should be accepted as a heritage. Any attempt to take over the originator's rights of authorship is a kind of usurpation that is doomed to failure. The congregation's collective memory of its origin will ratify it and bring it into the present.

This insistence on a conventual life modeled on older canonical forms has to be put in context with the issue of reconciliation. Such a life might also militate against the relaxing of cloister that Sophie Barat desired. On the other hand, *the spiritual aim of the primordial idea of the little Society* is properly incorporated. Always, the teachers must live in the presence of the risen Christ, be ready for action to make him known and loved "to the very ends of the earth."

II.2 Confirmation of the Initial Decisions

In 1814, Mme Barat installed herself in Amiens as superior general, sending Mme Baudemont to Poitiers. With Father Varin, she corrected the manuscript of the Constitutions that the Abbé de Saint-Estève had been working on for the past several years. The Ignatian character of it—a centralized government and mobility for its members—was clearly specified, as requested by the majority of the members of the Institute, and in keeping with the original plan of de Tournély.

The Abbé Sambucy de Saint-Estève seemed to accept this decision, but in fact, he in no way agreed with it. He had not abandoned his ambition of becoming superior general of an order calling itself "The United Ursulines." In 1815, he traveled to Rome and began a process of intimidation by mail, writing under the pseudonym of Stephanelli, a presumed Jesuit. He rallied the clergy of Poitiers to his cause. In addition, two religious from Amiens (one his biological sister) joined him, having faith in his grand scheme.

At the request of Father de Clorivière, and in close collaboration with Mme Barat and Joseph Varin, Julien Druilhet[62] wrote the new Constitutions, examined and adopted by the second General Council of the Institute that assembled in Paris from November 1 to December 17, 1815. The name *The Society of the Sacred Heart of Jesus* and the promulgation of the Constitutions brought stability and identity to the Institute. They officialized the Society's purpose of educational service.

In 1816, Mme Baudemont joined the Roman community of

---

62 Julien Druilhet was born July 8, 1768, in Orléans and died August 30, 1845, in Toulouse. He joined the Jesuit order in 1814.

the monastery of Saint-Denys. Against the wishes of its founder (the Abbé de Saint Estève), the new community was recognized by the pope simply as a "pious house" under the authority of the diocesan Ordinary, not as a religious order. And in this same year, through the mediation of Father Fontana[63] and the Abbé Perreau, the impostor, Saint-Estève, found himself finally unmasked.

To Discover the Love of the Heart of Christ

The Constitutions announced a new position within the educational community: the Mistress of Studies, another name for "the prefect" in the Company of Notre-Dame. Her function was to guide the studies of those religious destined for teaching, to oversee academic performance, and to supervise and counsel the classroom teachers. This choice strengthened the institution's adherence to the Jesuit model.

For the mistress general of the boarding school, the first rule makes clear the new religious Institute's spiritual orientation: "to work tirelessly for the glory of the Sacred Heart of Jesus, to form young hearts in his love, to employ learning only as a useful instrument for directing them toward this noble goal." This statement clearly expresses the intention of *The Provisional Plan of Study in Use at the House of Amiens*. The primary responsibility of the mistress general is to direct the students' thoughts toward discovering the love of Christ.

---

63 François-Louis Fontana was born in Casal-Maggiore, in the region of Milan, in 1750. He accompanied Pope Pius VII into France in the role of theologian. Imprisoned at Vincennes in 1811, he was liberated in 1814 and recalled to Rome by the pope, who made him a cardinal in March of 1816. He died in 1822.

The final rule (rule 44) invites her to bind herself to Christ when fatigue begins to overtake her: "Finally, in the moments when the mistress general finds herself overcome by the burden of her activities, she will cast an eye upon the Sacred Heart of Jesus, and will draw from it new strength for imitating this perfect model of zeal, patience, and charity."

These rules, 1–44, relate education to three points: Jesus Christ; the teachers; the students.

This triad can be found in the second rule for classroom teachers and supervisors.

"By All the Means within Their Power"
Teaching allows for a range of methods of instruction. The Constitutions formulate it this way: "The means used by the Society of the Sacred Heart to glorify the Heart of Jesus by working toward the sanctification of others are chiefly:
1. The education of young boarding students;
2. The free instruction of poor day students;
3. Retreats facilitated for lay people;
4. Necessary relationships with people from outside.[64]

The provision's use of the word *chiefly* opens the door to other possible ways of interacting, in line with the ultimate purpose of the Institute. From the Society's founding stages—from 1801 to 1826—the superior general followed this pattern when local situations required it. By this reasoning, the orphanage at Sainte-Pezenne was opened in Niort. The same thing happened in 1819 in Bordeaux, at the request of Mme de Lalanne. Centers for the

---

64 *Constitutions, Société du Sacré Cœur de Jésus, Institut de droit pontifical, Plan abrégé de l'Institut*, A. S-C. F, p. 18.

orthopedic treatment of motor disabilities were established in Paris and Lyon, as were workshops for professional formation in Grenoble and Beauvais. In Florissant, in the United States of America, Philippine Duchesne founded two schools of home management, one of which was for Native American girls.

This diversity continued past the early years. In 1832, following an epidemic of cholera, the Paris school received a dozen little girls aged eighteen months to five years whose mothers had died. The same thing happened in Rome in 1839 at the Santa Rufina school. In Marmoutier, near Tours, a day school for boys was opened. A few years later, an orphanage was established at Neuville-les-Amiens, then in Beauvais and Moulins, Charleville and Saint-Ferréol, Nancy and Kientzheim near Colmar, Jette-Saint-Pierre, near Brussels, and Blumenthal, near Aix-la-Chapelle; at the Villa Lante in Rome and in Lemberg, Poland; in Detroit, Michigan, and Sancti Spiritus, Cuba. At the house in Chambéry, on January 1, 1843, a center was established for deaf-mute children.

The Institute's first teacher training school opened in Pignerol, Piedmont, in December 1839. A second was founded in Santiago, Chile, at the request of the government in 1854. These institutes represented yet another form of *the primordial idea of the little Society*. The teachers passed on the sense of mission. At Pignerol, "in 1840 more than twelve hundred children owed to the devotion of these women the invaluable benefits of a Christian education." And at the college of Santiago: "Sixty of them spread out into the countryside are true apostles among their students, offering themselves as examples of fidelity to their religious duties, and attracting people's devotion to the divine

Heart of Christ in a thousand different ways."[65]

The coming together of teaching and spiritual direction took on a new dimension: "They maintain a useful and fruitful correspondence with their former schoolmistresses, and every year during their vacation, they come to re-immerse themselves in the Sacred Heart by making a retreat." In fact, social and spiritual aims are intrinsically linked in the original vision of Sophie Barat. They cannot be separated, at the risk of losing sight of the special feature that characterizes this educational plan. At its peak, culture aspires to produce a twofold effect, suited to both scholarship and practical life.

In this sense, intellectual formation is the necessary forerunner to the spreading of the Gospel. As Guy Avanzini[66] explained it during a colloquium on the educational tradition of the Society of the Sacred Heart: "for Madeleine-Sophie Barat, there is no contradiction between sanctity and culture. Rather, a robust culture can generate holiness."[67] According to the designs of the founders, the two associated elements are in fact only one. The spiritual goal implies intellectual development. And accordingly, the development of the intelligence is controlled by an awareness of the meaning of existence and the discovery of the presence of Christ in daily life. The founding charism joins—in a single convergence—educational action to a spiritual

---

65 Joséphine Gœtz, État de la Société du Sacré-Cœur en 1865, Paris, October 5, 1865, A.G.S-C., H-I, Transcription, p. 18.

66 Tr. Note: The original [French] edition of this book was published as part of a larger series of books on education directed by Guy Avanzini, a noted French educational scholar.

67 Guy Avanzini, La spécificité éducative de la Société du Sacré-Cœur, A. S-C. F, p. 4.

purpose. This is why the work of retreats and the sodalities[68] follows logically from the training of both day and boarding school students.

It sometimes happened that this "third way" was the only one chosen. This was the case in Riedenburg, near Bregenz, an establishment opened in 1854: "The retreats go on one after the other almost without interruption. Close to 700 people from every social class join in these holy Exercises where the graces of conversion fill them. The poor women living in the village or the surrounding area profit especially from this path to salvation; they come to the school, ten or twelve of them at a time, and one finds among them souls that are truly faithful, some of the best."[69] The same thing occurred in France at Laval, founded in 1841.

In addition, the Constitutions of 1815 do not limit the educational mission to young women. They extend it to the parents and anyone else who is welcomed in the "parlor." The Constitutions also call for it in the job description of the director of the poor school, through meetings with parents. Yet the importance of these "necessary relations with people from the outside" is far from minor. From a legal point of view, this course of action is unprecedented and governs "the likelihood of a broad openness in the future."[70]

This form of intervention required discernment, gentleness

---

68   The first Congregation of the Children of Mary was established in Amiens in 1816; in 1820, the same association began at the boarding school in Paris. See: Reverend Father Druilhet, *Aux enfants de Marie, Instructions pour leur servir de règle de conduite dans le monde*, Paris, Lib. Poussiègue frères, 1879.

69   État de la Société du Sacré-Cœur en 1865, p. 5.

70   J. de Charry, *Les Constitutions définitives et leur approbation par le Saint-Siège*, Part 2, Vol. I, Exposé historique, Rome, p. 155.

and firmness, goodness and patience, zeal and charity. As a guidebook then in use by the educators expresses it: "They discern with prudence what the age, rank and quality of a person will allow them to say for the glory of God and the good of her soul. There are those to whom they might give salutary advice and propose wise rules to guide them in the world, inspiring them with a disdain for vanities and fleeting pleasures; leading them toward certain spiritual practices such as meditation, the examination of conscience, spiritual reading, recourse to the Sacred Heart of Jesus and Mary in all their activities; and above all recommending that they avail themselves of the sacraments."[71]

From then on, the triad becomes:

Heart of Jesus	
draw from it	
this authentic love	
educators	students - parents -
	everyone from outside

When the institutional rapport between those "inside" and those "outside" begins to change, the apostolate will change as well.

In 1820, a General Council proceeded to evaluate the boarding school plan of studies. Would the original choices be ratified?

When Uniformity is Present at the General Council

A circular letter defines the goal of this third General Council as follows: "The Society having made several new foundations,

---

71 *Rapports avec les personnes du dehors*, Constitutions, Troisième partie, VI, ibid., p. 117.

and the rules established having been amended according to what was felt to be necessary for the greatest number of students, without having realized it we have begun to differ with respect to several items. And because one of our dearest hopes is to work to establish and conserve the uniformity of our establishments, it seems urgent to us, before the Society extends itself further, to consolidate the houses already established in regulating all that might contribute to their well-being—both spiritual and temporal."[72] The purpose of the anticipated convocation of the third General Council is explicit. The essential concern is to guarantee the uniform application of the directives found within the Plan of Studies and the rules for the boarding schools, in order to promote the expansion of the Society's work while also consolidating what is already in place.

Particular events underlay this decision. Liberties had been taken at the House of Amiens under the leadership of Mme Baudemont: students were allowed to leave the school grounds more often and academics suffered. In other places, particularly the Paris house, social visits were allowed, to the detriment of the girls' studies. But, more important, the houses of Beauvais and Grenoble had been asked to apply the method of mutual instruction whose guiding principle was the instruction of students by other students. A group of monitors, consisting of the best student in each class, took on the tasks of the teacher allowing a single teacher to direct an entire school.

The inventor of this monitorial system was Dr. Bell, an Anglican pastor. In 1798, in London, the Quaker J. Lancaster put it into practice in a primary school. This mutual instruction

---

72 Letter of convocation to the General Council, A.G.S-C, p. 1.

method saw a rapid rise in England and other English-speaking countries: the United States, Canada, Australia, and India. In 1814, in Paris, the *Society for Elementary Instruction* was founded. This group edited the *Practical Manual of the Mutual Instruction Method,* by which its use spread widely. A school was opened under the patronage of Carnot. The Prefect of Oise, the Count of Germiny, became a zealous promoter and planned to implement the method at the free school connected with the Sacred Heart boarding school in Beauvais, which had just fallen under his jurisdiction. On August 1, 1817, he courteously informed the Superior General of this fact, laying out his reasons and leaning for support on the agreement of his immediate superior, the Minister of the Interior.

The preceding June, Sophie Barat had received a message informing her of the prefect's intentions.[73] An exaggerated critique depicts the ideological conflicts between liberals and ultramontanes.[74] Faced with this ideological combat,[75] Sophie Barat chose the path of prudence and obedience to ecclesiastical authority. With tact and firmness, she responded to the prefect in the negative. Other letters followed. The prefect castigated the school's bias against any kind of innovation and underscored the need for the ecclesial authority to submit to that of the

---

73 June 25, 1817, *Lettre à la Supérieur d'une Communauté réligieuse qui tient des Ecoles de charité et à laquelle on propose d'adopter l'enseignement à la Lancastre,* unsigned letter, A. S-C.F, B.01.

74 Maurice Gontard, *Histoire mondiale de l'Education,* Vol III, edited by G. Mialeret and J. Vial, P.U.F., Paris, 1981, p. 254.

75 Tr note: The term *ultramontane* refers to those Catholics who favor centralizing Church power and authority in Rome. France (especially the French bishops) had been engaged in an ongoing power struggle with Rome since the Middle Ages. Sophie found herself caught in the middle of this age-old dispute on more than one occasion.

government. But Sophie Barat did not give in to this moral pressure: the mutual method of instruction drew much opposition, and its application would risk serious institutional damage. In 1819, she issued the same refusal to Thérèse Maillucheau, superior of the House of Grenoble.

In the face of these events, the watchword was "establish uniformity." This way of seeing things was an attitude inherited from earlier times. Dominique Julia highlights this feature of civilization in the eighteenth century: "As the century progressed, developers of educational plans increasingly saw uniformity as the best means of forging a national sentiment, molding citizens into countrymen, and opposing the one-upmanship behind proposals resulting from differing views on educational subject matter."[76]

This notion was shared by male religious congregations, where it is often expressed as a sectarian idea.[77] It can be found, too, in the educational rules of female Institutes that had adopted the teaching methods of the Jesuits. This was the case with the Ursulines, although each monastery had an autonomous government structure. The same recommendation was made by Pierre Fourier to the teachers of the Congregation of Notre-Dame.[78]

---

76 D. Julia, *Les trois couleurs du tableau noir, La Révolution*, Belin, Paris, 1981, p. 20.

77 J-B. Corbin, *Mémoire sur les principaux objets de l'éducation publique*, quoted by D. Julia, p. 21.

78 *Les vrayes Constitutions des Religieuses de la Congrégation Notre-Dame*, XII, 1694, Archives, Paris, p. 93.

This is the tradition that gave rise to Joseph Varin's exhortation to the opening session[79] of the third General Council in August of 1820. The speaker situates the task of the group within its own origins. Then he reformulates the objective of the assembly: "You have come here," he said, "in order to repair certain disruptions. But where do they come from? They may come from the Constitutions themselves, or from those individuals who interpret them, or from pressing circumstances. If the obstacles come from individuals, it is doubtless through an excess of zeal or good will. One might well believe that in order to achieve the greatest good, one needs to make a few changes. . . .Uniformity is so desirable that it is essential for you to unite in order to stabilize all that can be stabilized." On this point, as with the practice of religious virtues, the Jesuits were proposed as a model.

Nevertheless, experience quickly showed Mme Barat that uniformity does not strictly apply in every circumstance. The establishment of boarding schools in Savoy, Piedmont, and Louisiana brought home this idea. From 1819 on, the Superior General expressed this position to Philippine Duchesne regarding the rightness of the move from Saint Charles to Florissant: "I share with you my reflections and my concerns; I will not dictate a rule of conduct to you. It is only when one is physically on the premises that one can properly judge a situation."[80] In the same way, in 1820, she wrote regarding pedagogical choices: "I

---

79 *Journal de la Maison de Paris*, Notebook 1, *Retraite à Paris,* August 12, 1820, A.G. S-C, C.1.

80 Saint Madeleine-Sophie Barat to Saint Philippine Duchesne, *Correspondence*, Text presented by J. de Charry, letter 113, Paris, July 9, 1819, Rome, 1989, p. 232.

understand very well, after the explanation you have just given me, that it is hardly possible for you to follow the Plan of Studies. You must do the best you can and navigate your way towards it however you can."[81] She favored adapting standard textbooks to suit different mindsets and local educational demands.

Twenty years later, two letters demonstrate the same idea. The first is addressed to Eugénie de Gramont, just before the General Council of 1839. She insists on a judicious use of textbooks, depending on local issues: "I think that we will put the Plan of Studies aside until a bit later. We will construct the core, then each country can develop its own version, because for us, women, it seems impossible that things should be the same everywhere! The Education of women varies from nation to nation: in the north, it's work with one's hands; in the south, it's science; in Italy, a blending of the two; in Spain, it will be religion and very little science: and then it all depends more or less on the talents of the people involved. It seems impossible that this work can have identical applications from place to place, and upon our return to you, we will put one of our own in charge who best understands all of this."[82]

Sophie Barat made the same observation to Aimée d'Avenas, aware that the plan of studies had to be rewritten: "We will spend the year with our traditions and our experimentations, but we will put an end [to decisions]; impossible for that matter to achieve perfect uniformity everywhere. The groundwork having been established, it will be absolutely necessary to allow modifications to be made in the various countries where we are

---

81 Letter to Eugénie Audé, director of the House of Saint Michael, May 28, 1826, A.G.S-C, C-I, A I.

82 Letter of May 28, 1839, A.G.S-C, C-I, A I.-F Box II.

located."[83] What, then, is the groundwork to which she alludes? For Janet Erskine Stuart, sixth superior general of the Institute, it meant a foundation in philosophy and theology, allowing for a judicious variation when called for. She expressed it in these terms: "The Blessed Foundress herself, with the help of her advisers and of some experienced Jesuits who gave lectures to the communities, drew up the first program of studies.... The first framework has always been preserved, because with its cornerstone of religious knowledge and its well-proportioned foundations in the elements of philosophy, it is adaptable to whatever may be built upon these foundations."[84] This interpretation is aimed at one model, the Jesuit *Ratio Studiorum*.

The Hôtel Biron, Future "Fashionable Convent"

Before broaching the question of studies in the boarding schools, the General Council of 1820 studied the applications for new foundations. Their number reveals the mutual support of both the government and the ultramontane milieu. The written report gives these priorities as follows: "At the first gathering, our Mother presented us with a list of the foundations requested by the Bishops. We put all of this aside for a later time. We were convinced that we would accept only those where we were offered a house, a garden, etc. The foundation in Le Mans shows early promise, the one in Paris warrants every sacrifice."

One of the criteria for selecting an establishment was its spaciousness, essential because of cloister. The Institute

---

83 Letter of June 22, 1839, A.G.S-C, C-I, -F, Box X.
84 Janet Stuart, *La Société du Sacré-Cœur*, Roehampton, London, 1923, p. 88. J. Stuart is also the author of *The Education of Catholic Girls* (French edition, Paris, 1914).

considered the acquisition of the Hotel Biron, which then belonged to the Duchess of Charost.

The Journal of the Paris House relates the deliberation as follows: the property "offers all the advantages one could ever hope for and a space large enough for our establishment. It was unanimously decided that the Society would buy the Hotel Biron in order to create a headquarters for our Society." Financial help would be needed.

With this in mind, the Countess de Marbeuf, who had been accepted into the novitiate in this same year of 1820 after being widowed, was sent to the royal palace. "She made her way to the Tuileries and, alone, was given an audience with the king, who invited her to sit down. She expressed the desires of our Society, consecrated to a devotion that had been adopted in order to invite his restoration—hopes that had been fulfilled, because she had the pleasure now to see him before her. She made her request, gave him her address, which he read attentively, and he responded with good will that he would look into it and do whatever he could. She left as she had entered, her mantle trailing behind her, and making three bows according to the protocol of the court." But upon her return, she felt that she had been too timid and not persuasive enough. At the same time Mme de Gramont approached her brother-in-law, "the duke de Gramont, who immediately went to find Mr de Pradel, Secretary of State, in order to explain our appeal. Loans were arranged by Minister de Montmorency and Messrs. Laurent and Morand, of Amiens. The conditions required for the purchase of the Hotel Biron having been met,[85] the Institute took up the

---

85 The boarding school was transferred from the rue des Postes (today, rue Lhomond) to the Hotel Biron on October 4, 1820.

various requests for foundations: Le Mans, Auxerre, Soissons, Autun, and Bordeaux.

Any decision about studies was then delayed by the end-of-year examinations in boarding school in the rue des Postes. Msgr. Frayssinous, ecclesiastical superior of the Paris school, vicar general of the diocese, and Grand Master of the University, examined the girls who appeared at the Exercises on the subject of religion. On September 16, the distribution of prizes took place.

The Plan of Study is "Excellent"

The next day, a study of the boarding school regulations was finally up for discussion. It began with reports from the schools. The assembly was told that "we have not been completely successful" and it addressed the reasons why. Were the problems attributable to the plan then in use? After some deliberation, the following bill of health was delivered: "The Plan of Studies, with one small addition, has been declared excellent by all and so well analyzed that any lack of success has been due to students' unpreparedness or to teachers' failure to adhere to the plan." One wonders whether Jean-Nicolas Loriquet was behind this conclusion.

The Journal of the General Council reads: "Father Loriquet had the goodness to come to Amiens with Mother Prévost in order to deliver the decisions we needed for the Plan of Studies." In fact, he presided over the sessions with Msgr Frayssinous, Abbé Perreau,[86] and Father Varin, but given his role, it is not

---

86 The Abbé Perreau was a representative of Cardinal Périgord, Grand Almoner of France and at that time ecclesiastical superior of the Society of the Sacred Heart of Jesus. He presided at the General Council of 1820.

likely that he made that summary; a better candidate is Catherine de Charbonnel.

Better than anyone else, this experienced woman was in a position to present—in a clear and reasoned manner—the consistency of the Plan of Studies. Since the General Council of 1815, she had held a double position as first assistant general and bursar general. Her responsibilities gave her an overall view of the boarding schools and the quality of their instruction. Her appraisal—"We have not been completely successful"—corresponds to her objective and nuanced way of measuring the facts, without blaming those who were responsible for them.

Her biography supports this theory: "The third General Council of the Society gathered in Paris on August 12, 1820. Mother de Charbonnel left Lyon in order to attend. Aside from the official responsibilities that brought her there, her presence was required by more than her office: it was time to focus on the question of education, the studies themselves, and Mother Barat counted on the crucial contribution that her experience would bring to the discussion. Moreover, the depth of her wisdom made her particularly capable of writing the Plan of Studies, and Reverend Father Loriquet, who admired her enormously, did not fail to agree with Mother Barat on this point."[87]

If "We have not been completely successful," the lack of basic training of the teachers was at fault. The superior general regretted the situation and did not hesitate to emphasize it. By way of illustration, witness this rather sharp critique, addressed to Mme Michel, director of studies at the Grenoble school:

---

87 *Notice de la Révérende Mère de Charbonnel, Assistante et Econome générale de la Société du Sacré-Coeur de Jésus*, by M. Dufour, Rome, A.G.S-C, (1820-1822), p. 91.

"My dear Adrienne, by the way, you who are the mistress of studies, have you not noticed that several of your little ones, like Constance and Elisa, are languishing in the fifth class, repeating the same thing over and over and wasting their time? This thought does not come from me: I hardly think of these children; too bad if those in whose care I have placed them don't fulfill their duty! Talk about it with Mother Thérèse in the meantime, and look at the situation honestly."[88] What are the reasons for this?

Some of her religious were used to the older teaching methods of monastic educators—those of the Visitation Nuns, the Company of Saint Ursula, or Saint-Cyr. It was hard for them to adjust to a more advanced standard of teaching. Joseph Varin urged them to do so. Sophie Barat also recommended it and envisaged the creation of an upper level juniorate, which would train those religious who were destined to teach the "advanced classes."[89] but what *were* the corrections made to the *Plan of Studies of 1810* during the General Council of 1820? Did they harken back to the consistency of the original plan?

The changes dealt exclusively with the subject matter of the programs. There was a clear decision to return to the quality of instruction that had been present "from the beginning." The standard for progressing through the humanities was brought back. The level of instruction for the "lower classes" was fully restored to that of 1804. But, in the fourth class, the names of Bossuet and de Fleury were replaced by the acronym

---

88 *Lettre à Adrienne Michel, à Grenoble.* Paris, January 3, 1817, A.G.S-C, C-I, A I. G, Box 17.

89 This goal was not realized until 1865, under the leadership of Joséphine Goetz, second Superior General.

for Jean-Nicolas Loriquet, whose works became the required texts.[90] Secondly, the teaching of arithmetic brought together the concepts of "multiplication, long division, fractions, and geometric multiplication and division." Advanced instruction was no longer reserved for the first class but begun in the second class, where it was used to develop a sense of history. The instruction in the fourth and third classes prepared the way. The first class again studied poetry.

The educational goal was no longer the governing of a household and the acquisition of "good manners." Its chief objective was the students' independent judgment, as the reintroduction of graded humanities classes suggests. The norm of usefulness that had governed the writing of the Plan of Education for 1806 would from now on have to deal with that truth, the principle of making choices that would be consistent with the course of studies, as defined by the spiritual vision of the Institute. Yet biases persisted, as revealed by this recommendation of September 22, 1820: "Father Varin believes that we should rarely allow our students to study Latin, that we should try to keep them away from it, to be put off by it. Let us avoid the foolishness of creating femmes savantes."[91] Nevertheless, the direction established by the first community of Amiens was confirmed. The original convictions were ratified: education is accomplished through teaching; to know how to read and write is necessary in order to know how to think for oneself; to devote oneself to knowledge does not distance one from God, but rather allows one to find God.

---

90 Aimée d'Avenas, mistress general of the Paris boarding school and writer of several works on teaching, would fight this exclusiveness in vain.

91 *Journal de la Maison de Paris, Conseil général de 1820*, 4th notebook, A.G.S-C., C.I.

In the Footsteps of Saint Francis Xavier

On January 14, 1817, Mgr Louis Dubourg, Bishop of Louisiana and the two Floridas, asked for a foundation to be established in Saint Louis, Missouri. Sophie Barat thought the idea premature.

However, touched by the repeated pleas of Philippine Duchesne, she ended up giving her permission. And on March 21, 1818, "the little colony," composed of five religious including Philippine, embarked on the sailing ship *Rebecca*. After a perilous crossing, the missionaries arrived on May 30 in New Orleans, where they were received by the Ursulines. They made the trip up the Mississippi on a steamboat. In Saint Louis, a surprise awaited them: Bishop Dubourg had not arranged for them to establish a house there, as had been agreed. He sent them instead to Saint Charles, a town located at the border between the American territory and the Native American tribes. In addition, because of local social prejudices, they were not entrusted with the education of young Native American girls, but rather with that of young Americans.[92] The first girls' school west of the Mississippi, in Upper Louisiana, was opened on September 14, 1818. On October 3, a boarding school followed.

Thus, beginning in 1818, the international dimension suggested in Sophie Barat's *original idea* took concrete form. One by one, other schools followed: In 1821 in Grand Coteau in Lower Louisiana; in 1825 at Saint Michael, in 1828 at Bayou-la-Fourche; in 1827 in St. Louis, Missouri; and in 1828 again in Saint Charles.

---

92 *Philippine Duchesne et ses compagnes, Les années pionnières, 1818-1823*, Letters and journals gathered, prepared, and presented by C. Paisant, Cerf, Histoire, Paris, 2001, p. 26, Letter 54, p. 221.

A manuscript of thirty-four pages[93] takes a census of the houses of the Institute existing in 1827. It is entitled *Beginning of the Society of the Sacred Heart of Jesus in the Year 1801*. It offers a short history of each establishment, accompanied by an inventory of the premises. In most cases, the demand for a school arose from the local bishop. Sometimes, it came from parents of students or town dignitaries. Occasionally there was a merger with a small congregation.

The development of foundations might be represented as follows:

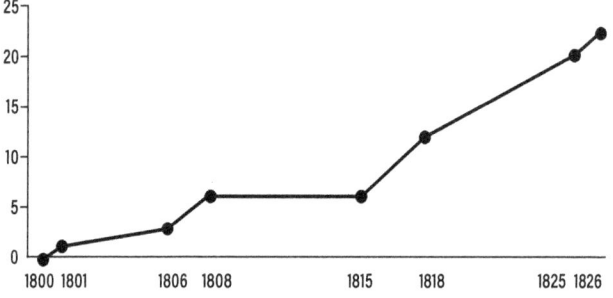

This upward curve represents the critical period of growth experienced between 1806 and 1815. The horizontal line corresponds to the overall growth of the Institute, paralleling that of other congregations with few differences. In fact, according to Claude Langlois, the growth of boarding schools run by teaching congregations flourished under the First Empire and even more so under the Restoration. Until 1850, this growth was steady. It accelerated under the first phase of the Second Empire because of the conservatism in families and a favorable

---

93 *Commencement de la Société du Sacré Cœur de Jésus en l'année 1801*, A.G.S-C, A-II, p. 33.

environment due to the Falloux Laws.[94] "Four surges are clear: 1805-1809, 1820-1829, 1835-1845, and finally 1850-1859."[95] In comparing this pattern to the general trend, the growth of the Society of the Sacred Heart is more apparent after 1815, with an accelerated rate between 1815 and 1820 and holding steady from 1820 to 1826. Three factors contributed to this growth: the return of the Bourbon kings, the restoration of the Jesuits in France, and the promulgation of the Constitutions of the Institute.

Except for What Does Not Agree with the Council of Trent

The House Journals of the various foundations show that relations with the outside world, between 1801 and 1815, were hardly those of monastic isolation. Even as she wanted a religious engagement that complied with solemn vows, Sophie Barat believed papal enclosure to be at odds with educational service. Thus, in Amiens, the teachers took the students to the cathedral for the Sunday services. On days of congé, they accompanied them to the Parc de la Hotoie or the Folie Binet, a small country house not far from the town. Professional resolve and spiritual demands determined these comings and goings. The point was to adapt the ordinary convent ways to the needs of the work at hand. From the moment she arrived in Grenoble, Sophie Barat demonstrated this goal by eliminating the traditional monastic grilles and choosing an approach to prayer that favored silence

---

94 Tr. note: The Falloux Law of 1850 gave legal status to independent secondary schools; it was seen as a way for the Roman Catholic Church to reestablish its earlier level of influence in education.

95 C. Langlois, *Le catholicisme au féminine, Les congrégations françaises à supérieure générale au XIXe siècle*, Quatrième partie, L'enracinement congréganiste, XIIIe, La dynamique des recrutements, Cerf, 1984, p. 529.

after one's work day. Such changes were not looked on favorably, however, and brought bitter criticism. The appearance of religious life and its interaction locally were not the practices of the Convent of the Visitation. Old ideas about this way of life, solidly rooted in the minds of the people, created a major obstacle to change.

That being said, the flexibility regarding cloister during the early years would diminish after 1815. This resulted from the recent institutional crisis and the means taken to overcome it, as was evident at the time of the boarding school's move from Cuignières to Beauvais, in 1816. In Cuignières, there had been engagement with the outer world. The school combined social interaction with the separateness required by spiritual life and teaching. It was still true in Beauvais when the school was dedicated, although back-pedaling soon set in. And the twenty-four students arriving from Cuignières found it hard to accept the changes to their lifestyle brought on by the rules of cloister. In 1818, social interaction with the outside world began to fall off, reverting to patterns of the old monastic schools.

As a result, certain limitations were placed on the ways education could be carried out. Free instruction for girls was no long assured within "neighborhoods named by the Mayor," as stipulated in the second clause of the municipal contract promulgated on September 1, 1815. Instruction was to take place within the convent walls. Unwillingly or not, the municipality accepted the rules of religious enclosure. Consequently, on August 8, 1821, based on the report of a special commission, the Municipal Council decided to purchase a house and garden, next to the boarding school, for the education of poor children. On November 21, the King approved its purchase by the Ladies of the Sacred Heart.⁹⁶ This reversal with regard to the outside world was less noticeable in Amiens, Poitiers, and Niort, where the style of life was more monastic than it was in Cuignières.

This backward turn arose from the desire to maintain older norms held by the students' families, the religious, and the clergy. Sophie Barat tried nevertheless to keep to her chosen course. And at the end of 1824, Abbé Perreau, the official delegate of Cardinal Caprara, ecclesiastical superior of the Society of the Sacred Heart, intervened on behalf of the Sacred Congregation of Religious Institutes to explain that papal enclosure is not compatible with education.

In spite of this official intervention, the concept of cloister continued to create difficulties and delay the approval of the Constitutions. As the Roman *rapporteur* notes: "In the proposed plan, such cloister is excluded because free access to the monastery is allowed to people from the outside; and for members of the society, freedom to move from one house to another is at the discretion of the superior, just as the superior herself may visit the other monasteries or delegate another person to visit them in her stead. All of this seems to contradict the unequivocal dispositions of canon law and the decisions of the Holy Council of Trent." The results were not long in coming. On December 22, 1826, the Constitutions were approved by Leo XII; the Society of the Sacred Heart was not termed an actual religious order, but a religious society. It would require simple vows whose distinction was that they were "perpetual conditional"⁹⁷ from the moment of first commitment, after

---

96 *Sur la fondation de Cuignières*, A. S-C. F., B-05, p. 27.
97 These perpetual conditional vows followed the Jesuit model.

the completion of the novitiate. Beginning in 1827, the rule of enclosure became permanent.

If the times favored feminine submission, a few American religious nevertheless put up some resistance. They thought that the new rules did not correspond to the needs of their families. Thus, in Grand Coteau, Louisiana, a boarding school run by Anna-Xavier Murphy, the educational community refused to follow the strict observance of cloister required in 1827 and deliberately opted to continue the previous practice. On January 20, 1830, Philippine Duchesne described the situation this way: "The house is like a beautiful secular home. We close the front door, but the side doors are left open, and anyone can come in easily and even walk around the house. The little children and the older classes leave cloister in order to walk through the woods or the meadows, where they are often to be found. We wish very much to preserve this practice, explaining that it is this openness that charms the parents and that the exercise of cloister is too restrictive."

This kind of thinking about norms coming from Europe was made clear in America beginning with the first foundation in Saint Charles, Missouri, where Bishop Dubourg and several nuns felt that the rules of cloister and the distinction between choir religious and coadjutrix[98] religious would be "incompatible with the 'pioneer' setting." These reservations arose from the encounter with new cultural paradigms: within a slave culture, such submission might appear as a counter-value "reserved" for black or Native American girls.

---

98 Tr. note: Until Vatican II, there were two levels of entry into the Society: "teaching" or "choir" religious, called Mother; and "coadjutrix" sisters, who served in menial capacities and were called Sister. See Footnote 12

At the same time, the Congregation of Saint Clothilde was being established on a more innovative model. In September 1820, Mme Desfontaines,[99] a former religious of the Monastery of Sainte Aure and director of the royal boarding school at Neuilly, met with Father Rauzan, superior of the Missions of France. They were in such agreement that the statutes of their future religious Institutes were soon drafted and approved on April 6, 1821, by Cardinal Périgord, Archbishop of Paris. The model of religious life replaced the image of a convent with that of a family. With this in mind, Archbishop de Quelen proposed that they take the name Saint Clothilde,[100] emphasizing a mother's ability to educate her children in the faith.

This contemporary attitude was reflected in their choice of secular dress and—and above all—in recruiting students. At the House of Neuilly, boarding students of aristocratic and middle class backgrounds lived together without major problems. To both groups, Antoinette Desfontaines managed to convey her opposition prejudices and her openness to contemporary life. Nevertheless, these new ideas met resistance from some priests, who could not accept the idea of a teaching congregation that was not cloistered, failed to distinguish its choir sisters, and did

---

99 Antoinette Desfontaines, a student and then a religious at the Monastery of Sainte Aure, understood well the persecutions of the Revolution. Supported by Father Delaleu, she opened a school in the rue de la Ceriseraie in 1801. In 1816, the boarding school was moved to the rue de Neuilly, with the designation of a Royal House.

100 Tr. note: Saint Clotilda was the second wife of Clovis, the Frankish king, founder of the Merovingian dynasty. She is given credit for the religious conversion of her husband and the spread of Christianity across the Western Europe.

not wear a distinctive habit.[101] The ecclesial culture of the time was not ready to accept the idea that women could be more independent and the style of religious life that corresponded with it.

Contrary to all of this, the rule of cloister, imposed by the Sacred Congregation of religious in 1826, would continue during a century and a half within the Society of the Sacred Heart. A tendency that was both restorational and ultramontane would conspire to keep it so. A manuscript[102] dated 1827 offers a window on the congregation's way of life at the time of the Restoration.

An Evocation of Origins

This account of the founding years is attributed to Mme de Gramont d'Aster.[103] The title suggests that there were four distinct and successive accounts.

Beginning of the 4 Societies
1. *The Fathers of the Faith, in Spoleto and in Rome.*
2. *The Fathers of the Sacred Heart, in Haguenfurt, Dilligen.*
3. *The Dilette di Gesù in Padua and in Rome.*
4. *The Religious Mesdames of the Sacred Heart of Jesus in Amiens, who were later approved by the Holy See in the year 1826.*

---

101 L. Foucher, *Madame Desfontaines et la Congrégation de Sainte-Clothilde de 1757 à nos jours,* Paris, Institut Sainte-Clotilde, 1965, p. 66.

102 *Commencements des 4 Sociétés*, AG. S-C., A-I-2) a)-b), p. 1.

103 Gabrielle Charlotte-Eugénie de Boisgelin (1766-1836), widow of the Duke of Gramont d'Aster, was a former lady-in-waiting to Queen Marie Antoinette of France.

The report is not correct. It actually follows the beginning and the development of the Institute of the Mesdames of the Sacred Heart through its pontifical approval. It recounts how its foundation is linked that that of three earlier Institutes: the two male societies and the Institute of the Dilette di Gesù. The document describes this process. It is in the form of a commentary consisting of a series of annotations, numbered from 1 to 33, which aim to "serve as clarifications for the notice published in three issues of the journal *The Friend of Religion*, by M. Picot."[104] These notes are followed by an "Excerpt from the Prophecies of Father Nectoux."

The purpose of Michel Picot's notice is clear from his title: "Historical Summary of Two Associations That Have Served to Reestablish the Jesuits." This article, dated October 4, 1826, describes the foundation of the Society of the Fathers of the Sacred Heart and the later association of Paccanarists. Also mentioned is the female Institute of the *Dilette*, specifically within the context of the protection accorded the Fathers of the Sacred Heart by the Archduchess Marianne, sister of the Emperor Francis II[105] and friend of Princess Louise de Bour-

---

104 M. Picot, *L'Ami de la Religion et du Roi, Journal ecclésiastique, politique et littéraire*, Vol. 49, Précis historique sur deux associations qui ont servi au rétablissement des Jésuites, Paris, Bibliothèque Nationale, notice no: FRBNF32691240.

105 Tr. note: Francis was the last Holy Roman Emperor, ruling from 1792 until 1806, when he was defeated by Napoleon and the Holy Roman Empire was dissolved. He was also the nephew of Marie Antoinette.

bon-Condé.[106] But there is no allusion made to the French Community founded in Paris on November 21, 1800. This omission prompted the editorial annotations.

The entire manuscript is centered on annotation #32, where the writing and promulgation of the 1815 Constitutions of the Society of the Sacred Heart are recalled. Capturing this moment in writing, as well as the growing pains leading up to it confirm what happened.

The process had three stages:
- the writing of the Constitutions of the Mesdames of the Sacred Heart;
- the acceptance of the Constitutions by the General Council of 1815;
- the reception and application of the Constitutions by the houses.

"Since this happy day, the Society of the Sacred Heart has spread and enjoyed further development, the number of their schools having rapidly increased. In 1827, there are sixteen in France, two in Piedmont, and three in Louisiana." However, "this happy day" evokes yet another: the return of the Bourbon kings. This plot had in fact two objectives: the restoration of the monarchy and the reinstatement of the Jesuits. But who, then, plays the role of our "Prince Charming"? It would seem to be Father Varin. And yet, might it not also be King Charles X? In other words, for whom is this story written? If the speaker is already identified, namely Michel Picot, who is the editor behind

---

106 The first attempt at establishing a female foundation was undertaken by L. de Tournély with Princess Louise de Bourbon-Condé.

the screen *really* addressing? There are two reasons to think that the purpose of this document was to speed up legal approval. The first is the dating of the manuscript— written after the ecclesiastical approbation, received from Leo XII on December 22, 1826, and before the definitive legal approbation, obtained by Royal Decree on April 22, 1827. The second indicator is the designation of the institute as a French Society, after clearly referencing its branches in Piedmont and Louisiana. Why was the Society's international dimension so subtly hidden? Why insist that the Society of the Sacred Heart had become French?

These annotations might well have been intended to favorably influence a definitive legal approval. The logic here is that the readership was largely aristocratic. Yet the Society's houses had received provisional legal authorization under the First Empire, and the governmental situation urged making the authorization permanent. The plan had furthermore been studied and ratified by the General Council of 1826. However, a second hypothesis is equally plausible: the "clarifications" brought to the attention of Michel Picot might also have aimed at the affiliation of the Society of the Mesdames with that of the Jesuits.

An official request for such an affiliation was addressed to the Jesuit superior general, Father Fortis, in 1828. Annotation 31's insistence on the Society's reliance on the Jesuits seems to have opened the door. The Society of the Sacred Heart owed its existence, its legal structure, its spirituality, and its teaching methods to them. These characteristics, "received" from the Jesuits, were invoked immediately after the Fathers of the Faith swore fidelity to de Tournély's project, as if to signify that the Society's identity emerged out of the original plan and became effective through the use of the name and the rules spelled out in the Jesuit model, as adapted to women. These two assumptions are thus plausible and not mutually exclusive.

This report essentially supports a double identity: Ignatian and French. It presents two contrasting positions: an openness to a modern way of life and a restorational, ultramontane ideology, reinforced by the return of the Bourbon monarchy. The second does not fail to support the emergence of schools in France, Italy, and the United States of America. And the declaration of Mme de Gramont d'Aster, affirming that the Society of the Sacred Heart has become French, might be considered indicative of a Gallican tendency—a harbinger of the second crisis that would rock the Institute twelve years later.[107]

At the end of this consideration of accounts of origin and founding educational plans, it would appear that the Society of the Mesdames of the Sacred Heart had several founders. Léonor de Tournély is the mystic at the very beginning of the plan; Joseph Varin is his plan manager. As far as Sophie Barat is concerned, *the original idea of the little Society* will guide her through storms and swamps. In a spirit of fidelity to the Church, with patience and a willingness to compromise, she will accomplish the task confided in her: to build the Society of the Sacred Heart according to the Ignatian apostolic model, with the dual goal of propagating the knowledge and love of Christ and mending the social fabric according to Christian values, by educating girls of the ruling classes.

---

107 On this subject, see: M. Luirard, *Madeleine-Sophie Barat*, Ch. III, Nouvelle Cité, 1999, p. 88-98; P. Kilroy, *Madeleine-Sophie Barat, Une vie*, Ch. 13-21, Cork University Press, Cork, Ireland, 2000.

The initial plan and its carrying out are centered on Scripture, the Heart of Christ, source of regeneration and tenderness, whose Good News" is to be communicated "to all nations." This biblical symbol is exemplified by the devotion to the Sacred Heart, prominent at the beginning of the nineteenth century and influenced by the spiritual movement of Paray-le-Monial.[108]

---

108 Tr. note: Paray-le-Monial is where Margaret Mary Alacoque experienced her series of visions of the Sacred Heart in the late seventeenth century.

CHAPTER III

The Distinctive Educational Purpose of the Society of the Sacred Heart

III.1 In the Ignatian Tradition of Educational Congregations

AMONG A VARIETY OF EDUCATIONAL STYLES, several female congregations founded during the Counter Reformation chose to use the pedagogical model of the *Ratio Studiorum*. The "Paris Method," adopted by the Jesuits, appeared in a number of rules that concerned both the organization of a plan of study and the management of a class. In different ways, these procedures could be found in the educational plans of the Company of Saint Ursula, the Congregation of Notre Dame, and the Company of Marie Notre Dame.[109]

Adapting to the Time and Place

Ignatius Loyola deliberately chose strong religious instruction

---

109 The Company of Saint Ursula was founded in Brescia by Angela de Merici in 1535; the Congregation of Notre Dame, Canonesses Regular of Saint Augustine by Alix Leclerc and Pierre Fourier, at Mattaincourt, Lorraine, in 1597; the Company of Marie Notre Dame, by Jeanne de Lestonnac, in Bordeaux in 1606.

whose goal was the formation of committed Christians. This choice underlay the educational projects of the convents of the Counter Reformation, supporting their goal to combat Protestant influence. Jeanne de Lestonnac planned to develop a religious order that would "teach Christian girls the truths and maxims of the Faith in the face of all heretical deceptions."[110] Angela de Merici had the same goal for the Ursulines. Instruction was designed to make the girls impermeable—like rocks—to the assaults of the Protestant polemic.[111] For the Congregation of Notre Dame, the Provisional Rule expresses the same goal, in language adapted to the intended audience.[112] In all cases, the major concern was ecclesiastical.

After the upheavals of the French Revolution, Sophie Barat established the same priority with her goal of "re-creating a solid faith foundation in souls." She was in essence extending a long Ignatian tradition, which responded to the ecclesiastical challenge of the moment: yesterday, heresy; today, godlessness. The first Religious of the Sacred Heart had known, in one way or another, the horrors of the Revolution. For a noble heart, the injustices suffered required an act of reparation that would not result in violent or shameful outcomes. Combat thus took a militant form and an ethical aim. The Mesdames of the Sacred Heart chose to commit themselves to a cause that would potentially—over the long term—restore Christian values.

It all too often happened, however, that parents were

---

110 Cited by F. Soury-Lavergne, p 136.

111 *Les Constitutions des Réligieuses Ursulines, Congrégation de Paris*, Ch. VI, Josse, Paris, 1705, p. 27-28.

112 *Extrait du règlement provisionnel, Congrégation Notre-Dame*, Archives générales, Paris, p. 1.

concerned only with their daughters' preparation for First Communion, as is clearly revealed in the Journal and Register of the Boarding School in Paris. Yielding to the families' wishes meant that only elementary catechetical instruction would be provided; that and the lack of further formation for the students were a common source of complaints in Sophie Barat's correspondence.

A second characteristic drawn from Jesuit pedagogy was placing a student at a learning level equal to her grasp of the rules of grammar. In the Ursuline monasteries, the principle used for the class levels was different. It linked, without specifying what they were, student capabilities with age and the number of students enrolled. In contrast, Pierre Fourier and Jeanne de Lestonnac adopted the organizing principle of the *Ratio Studiorum*. The division of students into classes was determined by their reading level, which would allow them to pursue other subjects.

- To ensure this result with the best organization, advantages and simplicity, the entire school will be divided into three classes.
- In the first will be those students who can read documents and other handwritten papers and letters.
- In the second, those who are learning to read printed books and who are already somewhat advanced in doing so.
- In the third, the primary students, who are beginning to learn their letters, put syllables together, and pronounce words.
- Those students in the first and second classes who would like to learn how to write will be taught to do so.

- Lessons in spelling, mathematics, and composition will be given only to the most advanced students in the first class.[113]

Jeanne de Lestonnac followed this progression. She added a condition for admission to a class: the structure and length of time given to drills. The plan called for four exercises: recitation, review of the preceding lesson, explication, and homework. It was de Lestonnac who structured the schedule of classes for boarders at the Company of Notre Dame.[114] Rule 16 of the Method of Classes stipulates weekly review.

Pierre Fourier also opted for this teaching method. He devoted an entire chapter of the Constitutions of the Canonesses of Saint Augustine to laying out "*the order and distribution of hours and exercises during class time*" for the students.[115] But here too, the method differs from that of the Ursuline Congregation of Paris in that it used only for the study of religion.

Diversified Scholarly Recruitment

Educational methods flow from the nature of their institutions. Because they responded to specific concerns, these orders for women addressed themselves to different clienteles. The Company of Saint Ursula served girls from the rural and urban lower middle class. Their recruitment set two priorities: catechetical training and preparation for the responsibilities

---

113 *Extrait du règlement provisionnel*, Chapters XII and XIII, p. 55 and 57.

114 F. Soury-Lavergne, *Chemin d'éducation sur les traces de Jeanne de Lestonnac, 1556-1640*, C.L.D., Chambray, p.p. 235-236, 247.

115 *Les Vrayes Constitutions de la Congrégation de Notre-Dame*, Troisième partie, XVIII, ibid., p. 85-89.

of running a home. The rules governing preparation for the sacraments were taken very seriously: 61 rules for the boarding students, 13 for the day students in the free schools.[116] The heated disputes between Protestants and Catholics called for "a need to offer solid instruction to children regarding Catholic doctrine, particularly concerning the sacraments." These rules coincided with the inauguration of the ritual of First Communion at the beginning of the seventeenth century. Doctrinal instruction was at a very elementary level; the student was called to the practice of the theological virtues. Other areas of study followed; in particular, care was given to teaching students how to write (codified in seven pages) and how to do various kinds of needlework (sewing, cross-stitch, tapestry, embroidery). This curriculum fit the educational mission of the monasteries of Saint Ursula: to form mothers of families who could care for a household and model the Gospel in their daily lives. In this way, it reinforced the educational mission: "to make religion a way of life."[117]

The Company of Notre Dame focused on an aristocratic population. Its project sought to train women who were more committed, "capable of defending their faith and sharing it through their speech as well as their actions." It mattered, therefore, that they be prepared to refute the heretical ideas. With this goal in mind, the program[118] integrated religious instruction, "arithmetic, the decoding of contracts, reading various books," and civility. The virtue prized above all was honesty. This term

---

116 *Règlements des Réligieuses Ursulines de la Congrégation de Paris, Livre I*, L. Josse, Paris, 1705, p. 44-48, p. 162-165.

117 Chantal Geudré, *Catherine Ranqué, une éducatrice*, Archives de Paris, p. 261.

118 F. Soury-Lavergne, p. 240.

was to be understood in a particular sense: "to be able to discuss morality, to write a letter or sustain a conversation in terms of the choices to be made."[119] The goal was to facilitate interpersonal relations, to develop the capacity to assert one's own rights, and to respect those of others.

To prepare women to have an effect on and transform their environment was a goal common to Jeanne de Lestonnac and Alix Leclerc, even if the two Orders addressed themselves to girls from different social milieus. Working with the poor was, in fact, considered "the essential and principal work" for the Congregation of Notre Dame, one of whose goals was the training of future teachers. In the Provisional Regulations, this project was made explicit: "By means of good instruction that is scrupulous and faithful, peace, repose, obedience to and fear of God will be instilled by all the houses that will be directed by women themselves trained in such schools (. . .) thus assuring that all the young girls will be taught in the same way."[120]

On the other hand, the societal issue behind the opening of a school of the Society of the Sacred Heart was the education of young women from leading families. This central choice was ratified by the General Council of 1826. Schools for the poor were not, except in unusual circumstances, founded separately. In this sense, the population to which the Society of the Sacred Heart addressed itself is closer to that of Jeanne de Lestonnac. However, a free school was almost always attached to a boarding school; one rarely developed without the other. One reason for

---

119 O. Gréart, p. 31.

120 *Extrait de quelques articles du règlement provisionnel que gardait les Filles de la Congrégation Notre-Dame avant qu'elles fussent religieuses,* Archives générales, Paris, p 1-2.

this choice was a spiritual one: the preference of Jesus Christ for the poor. If the latter were present in the educational plans of the monastic schools, a distinctive note was sounded in the rules for the boarding schools of the Society of the Sacred Heart.

Christ Alive in the Faces of the Poor

Boarders were required to exhibit a "lively faith" in their interactions with the day students. They were to bring the same reverence they brought to their veneration of the Eucharist to seeing the presence of Christ in the faces of the poor. The following rule is a genuine pearl from the original plan:

> The administrator and the treasurer for the poor school will see their role with respect to the poor as the most beautiful of their rights and responsibilities. What more noble, what sweeter privilege than to be the custodians and dispensers of the wellbeing of their companions? It is thus with a lively faith that they must fulfill their duties, always seeing in the person of the poor the person of Jesus Christ, and convincing themselves that the poor children confided to their care, children whom Jesus Christ always honored with His favor, should be even more precious in their zeal.[121]

To this ultimate educational end was added that of social justice. If educating the boarding students helped to pay the expenses of the day school, likewise, having the free school encouraged the development of a social conscience. The school rule put it in these terms: "We will, if at all possible, come to

---

121 *Règlement général des pensionnats du Sacré Cœur*, p. 127, 1820, A.G.S-C, Library M. Educ.

the aid of the very poorest: we will in this way channel the good will and devotion of the boarding students."[122] And the General Rules for the Boarding School specified two commitments owed to the day students on the day of their First Communion at their parish, and on the day of the solemn distribution of prizes on July 19. The responsibilities of "the administrator and treasurer of the poor school" had two objectives: "to direct every means of instruction and spirituality toward the salvation of their souls, and to distribute gladly the largesse that they would otherwise have realized from their meager work and savings."

Therefore, it was not simply a question of awakening a social conscience, but of offering an opportunity for spiritual and moral lessons. Such exercises prepared them for a committed Christian life. In this sense, the educational style of the Sacred Heart boarding schools followed Jeanne de Lestonnac's plan. But a spiritual and missionary purpose was expressed in an original way within the rules for the administrators and treasurers: these young women are called to be "living images" of the goodness and mercy of God, to inspire "compassion and zeal" in their companions with respect to the poor. This educational goal is present in Sophie's original project.[123]

When Intelligence and Compassion Go Hand in Hand

In various ways, competition was a conventional practice within all the teaching monasteries. The use of a system of "teams" was common in the schools run by the Company of Notre

---

122 *Constitutions et règles de la Société du Sacré-Cœur*, Règlement de l'école des pauvres, Paris, 1828, p. 93.

123 Its formulation will again be found, almost verbatim, in the guidelines elaborated after Vatican II.

Dame and by the Canonesses of Saint Augustine. The same thing applied to examinations and promotions. The practice of organizing a class into groups of twelve, according to the Jesuit model, was followed by Jeanne de Lestonnac. This appears in rules 12 through 14 of the *Formula for Classes*.[124]

On this point, the educational project of the Society of the Sacred Heart had its own practice of competition, as shown by this statement on routine rewards: "In the case of competition, when there is a contest between students, the victorious competitor wins points at the expense of the defeated one." Other forms of competition were promoted: honorary positions and prizes. The rule for choosing candidates matched the educational approach. It was phrased as follows: "These responsibilities are to the best-behaved and most advanced students, and we typically choose those who combine intelligence with faith."[125]

Such competition applied to several categories, including singing, the library, the sacristy, games, orderliness in the refectory, classes, and studies. In this way, particularly for the older students, competition called forth a sense of responsibility. The roles were redistributed each trimester in order to include the greatest number. In this way, the boarding school rules produced a model of an educational community where motivation, self-direction, and spiritual encouragement developed in the students, in close collaboration with the teachers. The prizes that all classes shared were those of wisdom and success, of diligence, and of excellence. Their raison d'être was "to reward merit and inspire a dignified rivalry." The educational plan for

---

124 F. Soury-Lavergne, p. 364.

125 *Règlement des pensionnats de la Société du Sacré-Coeur, 2e partie, art. 8,* A.G.S-C., D-I, p. 53.

Sacred Heart boarding students follows in a long tradition of women's education that had adopted the pedagogical model of the *Ratio Studiorum*. Its missionary goal was its own, but its pedagogical ideas corresponded to those of Jeanne de Lestonnac and Pierre Fourier.

The Educational Model of Pierre Fourier

The educational text for the day students of Lorraine is analogous to the *Plan of Study of 1804*.

The two projects have a similar structure.

Congregation of Notre Dame (1694)
Part III
Ch. V.	Teaching content for day students
Ch VI	Methodology
Ch VII	Way of teaching and learning
Ch VIII	Catechism and doctrine
Ch IX	Christian Instruction
Ch X	Civic and moral instruction
Ch XI	Reading
Ch XII	Writing
Ch XIII	Spelling
Ch XIV	Arithmetic
Ch XV	Manual work

Amiens Plan of Studies (1804)

Ch. I. Art 1.	Distribution of time
Art 2.	Division of classes
Art 3	Teaching (5th, 4th, 3rd, 2nd, 1st, Superior Class)
Ch II	Admission into classes
Ch III	Distribution of time
Ch IV	Recitation of lessons
Ch V	Correction of homework
Ch VI	Reading
Ch VII	French grammar and spelling
Ch VIII	History
Ch IX	Geography
Ch X	Literature

Chapter VI, "Methodology," explains the rule for admission into the free school of day students at Lorraine. If the subject matter is different, the organization of the text is similar. The only structural variation concerns the placement of the key parameter, "Order of Exercises and the Distribution of Time," situated at the end of didactics. But this pedagogical progression had already been explained in Chapter VII, "Ways of Teaching and Learning Prayers." This inclusion defines, in the Constitutions, the educational textbook for the day students.[126]

To be sure, the level of competence is different, but the understanding of the learning process is similar. In addition, the final objective corresponds to that of the third class in the 1804 Plan of Study: to be able to write a letter correctly. A few

---

126 *Les vrayes Constitutions des Religieuses de la Congrégation de Nostre Dame*, Troisième partie, De l'instruction des filles séculières, Des écolières externs, Toul, 1694, A.G., p. 24, 57.

examples are offered: "to write a short message to one of their companions, in order to exhort her to go to confession or to accomplish good works; or to congratulate her for something good that she has done or received; or to console or thank her. They should also be able to take up subjects that will have practical and suitable application for a young woman of the world." Instruction was meant to cultivate the ability to communicate well and to transmit Christian values.

Pierre Fourier's textbook might have inspired the writing of the Provisional Plan of Studies in use at the boarding schools. But did the same thing apply to teaching orphans and day students?

Appropriate for Day Students

In order to answer this question, we must consider three documents: the regulations for the poor school, the abridged plan for the school, and the regulations for the orphans. The first of these was the subject of twelve pages in the Constitutions of 1815, addressing the organization of the school and its teaching methods. As in the boarding schools, the Mistress General was charged with the admission of students and relations with the parents. Responsible for carrying out the educational goals and preparation for the sacraments, she was also in charge of religious instruction. She supervised the health of the teachers, the cleanliness and tidiness of the school, and the behavior and morality of the students. Director of the establishment, she acted in concert with the local Superior and the parish priests.

The abridged plan for the poor school,[127] consisting of fifteen

---

127 The prayer *Cœur de Jésus*, recited at the beginning of the morning lessons, situates it after 1815.

pages, is written in a literary style that allows us a better glimpse of the life of the day students. It standardizes the comings and goings to and from the school, the allotment of time, and the order of scholastic exercises. It delineates the rules for admission into the different levels of writing and arithmetic classes. It prescribes certain methods of instruction to be followed and describes the method for teaching the catechism. And it ends with a short set of school regulations.

The simplicity of the day school students' arrival contrasted with the complexity and minutiae of the rules of cloister at the educational monasteries. Above all else, the ritual of welcoming underlined the institutional identity. Morning and evening, after they entered the courtyard, the girls "advanced two by two to greet the statue of Christ placed at the end of the corridor." The same thing held for the final invocation of morning prayer: "Heart of Jesus, make it my part to love you always and always more."[128] While this prayer, repeated during the day, is addressed to Christ, at the convents of the Ursulines, the Sisters of Notre Dame, and the Canonesses of Saint Augustine, the invocation was made to Our Lady or to a patron saint.

Other practices reflected those of monastic education: the reading of the morning prayer by a student appointed to the task for a week, the division of each class into two groups, the length of classes, the alternation of scholarly exercises with manual work.

---

128 *Plan abrégé de l'école des pauvres,* A.G.S-C., D-I, Rome, p. 2.

The daily schedule or *"order of day"* was as follows:
Morning
7:15   Mass
7:45   Breakfast
8:30   Manual Work
9:00   Classes
10:30   Work, in two groups

Afternoon
12:00   Lunch
12:30   Recreation with needlework
1:30   Chapel, in two groups
2:00   Classes
3:00   Instruction, in two groups
4:00   Prayer and departure with leaders

The length of classes was one hour, morning and evening; added to that was a half hour of religious instruction in the afternoon. The day students were divided into three classes according to their reading level, a requirement found in Pierre Fourier's writing. The morning class was reserved for reading for the beginning and intermediate students, or for the study of catechism and a summary of Church History for the intermediate and oldest students. The key parameter—*the order and allotment of time for study*—is found only in the *Abridged Plan for the Poor School.* In the book of Constitutions, Article III of the Regulations limits itself to saying: "The shortest, clearest, and most communal approach must always be used in the instruction of poor children." The mistress general was charged with overseeing this and making certain that no innovations were made. What, then, is the method indicated by the word "communal"?

The Abridged Plan recommended a division of classes according to the level of instruction. The rule for admission was the same as that articulated by Pierre Fourier: "Our policy is not to admit students into writing classes if they don't yet know how to read, and not to teach arithmetic except to those who already know how to write." The teaching of catechism essentially resorted to memorization. The order of exercises followed this format:[129]

1. review of lessons
2. new lesson
3. other learning: a half hour of writing; a half hour of arithmetic; a half-hour of reading.

Weekly review was also a common practice. The essential difference had to do with the *Order of Exercises*, whose application appeared to be more flexible.

The forms of competition followed those of the boarding school: end-of-year exams, prizes and rewards, honorary responsibilities. The *Journal* of the Grenoble house mentions that for the day students: "One distributes grades and merit points, prizes and medals, just as we do for the boarding students. Their big festival is on July 19, the feast of Saint Vincent de Paul. On the day of their First Communion, when they are not in church, they spend time at the school, where students who have received honors make it their duty to receive them."[130] Responsibilities

---

129 *Plan abrégé de l'école des pauvres*, A.G.S-C, D-I.

130 *Journal de la Maison de Grenoble* (December 13, 1804 – December 27, 1813), written by P. Duchesne, A.G.S-C., A-II, p. 21.

were assigned: to accompany students in groups, morning and evening, into their neighborhoods; to distribute the thimbles and needles during sewing classes, or pens and models for the writing class. Overall, these practices seem to follow those of the boarding school. But was it the same for instruction?

The method for teaching reading fostered both attention and competition. For beginning students, instruction resorted to letters and syllables up on the blackboard; for the rest of the students, books designed for the program were used:

> One never had a student read any more than seven lines, sometimes fewer, so as to move quickly to the next student, in order to make certain that all were reading with their eyes and pronouncing very softly. When a student made an error, the teacher called on others until the word was read properly. The teacher did not intervene unless no one in the class could correct the error.

The teaching of writing was based on copying. Special care was given over to the models: "We will take care that the models students are given to copy contain nothing that isn't edifying or instructive." The same method can be found in chapter XII of the educational textbook for day students in Lorraine.

To judge from the instructions found in the *Abridged Plan for the Poor School*, the recommended method for teaching religion was the traditional one of question and answer. Those who could read learned their catechism at home. For the rest, the review took place twice a week, during class. For everyone, a general review took place on Saturdays. This teaching method called activities that invoked the student's imagination and sensitivity, such as "religious tableaux, devotional imagery, maxims, and hymns." Interiorization and practical application were encouraged, in a way that was both simple and easy to understand. The process suited its goal: "to reveal and to enjoy" the biblical message. "The young teachers will observe one another in order to internalize all of their lessons and discussions, but without anything mannered, stressful, or strained." In this way, religious training would simply be absorbed so that, "nourished with the purest milk of religion, the poor students would become Christians without realizing it."

If the language is no longer that of the seventeenth century, the intentions are not far from those of Pierre Fourier, who recommended never boring the students and advised respecting their own pace and rhythm. The process clearly retains Ignatian accents: it is a question of "revealing and enjoying" the mysteries and truths of the Christian faith. And for the afternoon instruction, proportionate to the students' age and intelligence, the goal was to see them "believe little by little in the Lord" and in the practice of virtue. In the same way, during the preparation for First Communion, spiritual instruction aimed to "touch" and to "penetrate above all else their hearts." At stake is a spiritual experience geared to building a life of faith.

However, the teaching of writing remained elementary, its standards far below those of Pierre Fourier and Alix Leclerc. The best students received "some light smattering of writing instruction, either by having them copy exactly pieces of writing that were well written, or by verbally explaining to them the simplest elements of grammar." By contrast, the Constitutions of the Congregation of Notre Dame, written in the 17th century, manifested considerably more ambition in the education of day students. There, students were taught general rules concerning nouns and their gender, the writing of words and their homonyms, punctuation, and pronunciation. These educational supports prepared them to exercise their future responsibilities: the teacher "will give them writing assignments such as various forms of receipts, vouchers, bookkeeping for merchandise sold, work provided, or money loaned, and for various other things, which one would ordinarily encounter in the world of business, and which should be put down in writing for security. She will show them the way to write distinctly, item by item, to tally the amounts for each, to calculate large amounts of money, and thereby become familiar with all kinds of transactions they might be required to handle."

Responding to the particular needs of their time and place, Pierre Fourier had as his goal the advancement—through education—of young girls of modest means. There, too, he was an innovator.[131] With a keen awareness of human dignity, his ventures aimed at bringing about biblical justice, instituting social relationships where children of disparate economic backgrounds could be brought together on the same social level. To assure the dignity of everyone was his goal; scholarly pursuits, which opened the way to employment, were his methods.

The plan of the Sacred Heart schools corresponded rather to that of the monasteries of Saint Ursula, whose social orientation was toward order and stability.[132] However, competence in learning was also a goal in the education of the orphans at the schools of the Sacred Heart, as indicated by this diagram of the program:

---

131 Before J-B. de la Salle, P. Fourier was the first to advocate the use of a blackboard.

132 Philippe Annaert, *Les Collèges en féminine, Les Ursulines,* C.D.R.R., Vie consacrée, 1992, p. 141.

Division of classes	Two classes in which students are divided according to age and aptitude.
Religion	Learn by heart and understand in proportion to intelligence the shorter catechism of the diocese. For those with more learning, the longer catechism of Malines.
Subjects	• Reading, writing, spelling, arithmetic. • Some understanding of religious history and geography.
Needlework	• Hemming and mending of fabrics, including silk. • Cutting out and sewing of shirts and dresses.
Domestic Work	• Washing, ironing, dressing, and coiffure. • Housekeeping.

Where the method is that of the *Abridged Plan for the Poor School*, the teaching is far more advanced. It includes concepts of general culture and aims to have students acquire competence in this area.[133] Upon leaving the orphanage, the goal was that the young woman would be prepared to function either as a housekeeper or as manager of her own household.[134]

At the school, whether it was the orphanage or the boarding school, the educational goal was personal growth and commitment. The means to that end were more intellectual for one group, more practical for the other. But for both groups, the means were guided towards a spiritual goal: to awaken students to the active presence of Christ and contribute to making him known through a variety of commitments.

These observations reveal that the organization of classes and methods of teaching were inspired by earlier educational models. The distinctive quality of the Plan of Studies for day

---

133 *Règlement des orphélines*, Beauvais, A.G.S-C., D-I, p. 20.

134 These occupational skills were typical of the school on the Rue Babylone in Paris. Cf. *L'Observateur français*, Tuesday, July 12, 1887, AGSC D-1.

students and orphans at the Schools of the Sacred Heart arises from the proposed scriptural model. Students were invited to imitate the virtues of obedience and submission to the Child Jesus.

The Plan of Studies Is Recommended to Other Institutes

The pedagogical practices in the boarding and day schools of the Society of the Sacred Heart drew on the feminine practices that were inspired by the Jesuit *Ratio Studiorum*. It is logical then that the Canonesses of Saint Augustine were, in their turn, easily able to adapt the advances made in the Plan of Studies of 1804. Events conspired to make this happen: the transfer of their convent in the rue des Bernardins to the Hôtel de Mory, in the rue de Sèvres, on July 2, 1818. The new quarters called for a different kind of student recruitment. According to the memoirs of the Convent des Oiseaux,[135] the boarding school students now belonged to "a more distinguished class than they had at the beginning, and their education demanded more attention."

In order to adapt to this situation, and on the advice of Fathers Varin and Druilhet, the school's director, Mother Marie-Sophie, asked the superior at Amiens to share her educational plan.

Madame Prévost, such a stranger to the little jealousies that can occur between religious Orders—all too common even in the most fervent houses and yet so unworthy of any heart on fire for the glory of God—said that she would be charmed to render us this service. In addition, she lent

---

135 The name, literally "Convent of the Birds," comes from the aviaries installed by Pigalle, proprietor of the Hôtel de Mory until 1785.

us the regulations for the boarding school and those of the congregations, and the two religious who accompanied Our Mother will copy them quickly. At the same time, Madame Prévost spent the greater part of a day with Our Mother, explaining the kinds of competition used in the Order's schools, and answering all of her questions.[136]

At the Convent des Oiseaux, changes were quickly put in place. They concerned the daily schedule, the length of the school year, and the plan of studies. The superior class was added, as well as the honorary responsibilities. Students from the sixth class through the superior class who had achieved distinction, like those at the Sacred Heart, wore wide, colored ribbons over the shoulder. And in 1823, an association honoring the Sacred Heart was established. Life at the boarding school of the Oiseaux was restructured to follow the educational model of the Society of the Sacred Heart. The report was written with a respect that demonstrated both cleverness and spirit: "So that we can now say that it is due to their kindness and their zeal that the house owes the regard it enjoys today." The writer seems to ignore the fact that, twenty years earlier, the same thing had happened, going in the other direction, to the advantage of the Mesdames of the Sacred Heart.

Later, about 1860, the Plan of Studies for the Sacred Heart boarding schools must have been transmitted to the Company of Notre Dame. Françoise Soury-Lavergne highlighted the existence, "in the 19th century, of an elaborate internal set of rules

---

136 *Mémoires du Couvent des Oiseaux*, Archives générales de la Congrégation Notre-Dame, Paris, p. 232-280.

dealing with how to administer the educational institution."[137] This document has two parts. The first develops the rules; its introduction is written in terms identical to those of the General Rule for the boarding schools of the Sacred Heart.

A second part is titled "Plan of Study." The bibliographic references, the course of studies, and the method all follow the model of the textbook drawn up by Jean-Nicolas Loriquet in 1804 for the first Sacred Heart boarding school. History and literature were graded.

Schooling extends from the seventh class to the first class. An additional class follows the first: "The essential goal of this year is to adopt ideas of Christian philosophy drawn from excellent writers who, in affirming their faith, help the students resist the seductive torrent they will encounter in going out into the world. They will read serious and instructive works, Rollin's *History*, according to Lebeau, Lhomond, etc. They will learn and analyze Bossuet's *Discourse on Universal History*. They will follow a short course on logic and fine oratory. They will study botany and the celestial sphere, they will summarize a religious work at their level." In its structure and content, the Rule at the school at Albi is closer to the Plan of Studies of the boarding schools of the Society of the Sacred Heart than it is to the Rules for the Company of Notre Dame of 1638.

The original educational plan of the Society of the Sacred Heart drew its major components from monastic education, but its significant innovation was its advanced teaching methods. The decision was bold because it corresponded with an image of women that the conservative milieu of the era was not ready to accept.

---

137 See the chart elaborated by F. Soury-Lavergne, p. 334-335.

Nevertheless, a path had opened up, and the Canonesses of Saint Augustine and the Sisters of Notre Dame followed suit a few years later. Inheritors of the *Ratio Studiorum*, these groups of educators and the Religious of the Sacred Heart were in place to help one another at different moments in their history.

III. 2 In Imitation of the Heart of Christ

The interweaving of social and ecclesial purposes is clear from the degree to which the different educational projects adopted Jesuit pedagogy. Development was always a prominent goal—to prepare young women who would be committed members of their social environment and effective witnesses to the Gospel. Nevertheless, if each Institute aimed to humanize social interactions through the influence of women, it addressed itself in a particular way to a given social milieu. And it gathered its energy from its own charism—that is to say, from a very specific evangelical appeal that appeared in its ethical choices. As Guy Avanzini has pointed out, it is these educational aims[138] that prepare students for a way of being in the world.

We must pause here to examine this heritage before we can investigate the transformations realized by the Society of the Sacred Heart at the end of the twentieth century, and thus be able to appreciate them.

Simplicity to Be Safeguarded

The societal goal of the Ursuline Congregation of Paris is made explicit in its Constitutions. The monastery is conceived and designed to offer a good Christian education to young girls in

---

138 Guy Avanzini, *Introduction aux sciences de l'éducation*, Privat, 1987, p. 92-93.

the secular world. The uniqueness of the project is described as follows: "In these times, iniquity abounds and corruption of morals extends itself even into the very young."[139] Within its historical context, Angela Merici's initiative is responding to the challenge launched by the Reformed Church. It is expressed through "the desire and resolution to give ourselves over to the instruction of young girls, in order to help them conserve the grace of their baptism, fountain of all goodness, and to provide growth and increase." The educational activity is ordered toward this goal. The welcoming of a boarding student makes it clear from the start. From the moment of her arrival, the student is invited to renew her baptismal promises, modeling herself on Saint Ursula, virgin martyr.

The charter sets forth the main goal: independence of judgment or self-determination. Embedded throughout the text of the Constitutions, this educational goal takes shape in the Rule with several specifications concerning how classroom space is distributed, choice of subjects taught, and the process for recruiting students.

The first chapter of Book I of the Constitutions demonstrates an orderly environment where each class has its own place for its young scholars and their pious activities. The number of students is limited to no more than twenty per class. The distribution of space could be found in the organizational chart of the institution where rooms were assigned according to duties. The Order sought to provide an education that would ensure fidelity to the baptismal promises.

---

[139] *Règlements des Religieuses ursulines de la Congrégation de Paris*, Livre premier, Première partie, Chap. I, art. 1.

In order to accomplish this goal, the students had to be schooled in as much independence of thought and action as were available to women. Catechetical instruction contributed to this, helping students to develop their religious practice and safeguard their baptismal promise. In the same way, reading, writing, and arithmetic opened the way to a certain independence of action. Learning to sew, tailor, and do needlework supported that independence, positioning a young woman to make an "honest" living.

This training prepared her to assume the future responsibilities of homemaker and mother. It aimed to maintain and develop a certain self-dependence—specifically, an integrity of thought and action. This was the way of life for which a student of Saint Ursula was prepared. Shaped by the concerns of a Catholic Reconquest, she took as her model the Institute's patron saint.

With Honesty, in the Image of Our Lady
The same ecclesiastical concerns led Jeanne de Lestonnac to found a new religious order, although her motives were more personal. The daughter of Richard de Lestonnac, she herself had experienced, within her own family, the Catholic-Protestant division. In addition, her worldly experience in society had allowed her to appreciate the influence of women on their immediate surroundings. This experience, linked with a humanist culture, made her aware of a contemporary need: the importance of a Catholic institution for the education of girls in the province of Bordeaux.

Jeanne de Lestonnac envisaged the "creation of a work in which women would not be afraid to speak out and to open up the treasures of knowledge to future mothers of families."[140] A plan to build this work was developed in stages. On March 7, 1606, she wrote of it to Cardinal de Sourdis under the title: "Summary or Format of the Institute for Religious Girls of the Glorious Virgin Mary, Our Lady." She argued that the project was necessary. And in the face of resistance from the prelate, she highlighted the goal: to instruct "Christian girls about the truths and maxims of the faith against the trickery of the heretics." The challenge was set. The Order's goal was defined.

In this proposal, the Virgin Mary has the place of honor—a person to be admired.[141] If the educational project of the Canonesses of Saint Augustine invites one to imitate the effective tact and self-effacement of Our Lady in order to proclaim divine mercy; that of Jeanne de Lestonnac centers, rather, on interiority and simplicity. Such attitudes favor the calm self-assurance required to affirm one's convictions and respond to one's faith. To accomplish this mission, the formation of judgment is essential, as is access to the liberal arts/humanities. The *Quatrains* of Pibrac serve as a school of wisdom. These counsels of civility safeguarded students from the frivolity, corruption, and hypocrisy. They urged a certain freedom within friendship.

The ethic of relationships, based on respect for the other as well as oneself, had honesty as its core, meaning "that which deserves to be honored." Its practice helped to strengthen the moral fiber of families and society and to foster social harmony. Only with good judgment could it succeed. Based

---

140 F. Soury-Lavergne, *Chemin d'éducation sur les traces de Jeanne de Lestonnac, 1556-1640*, C.L.D., Rome, 1984, p. 77-80, p. 136.

141 F. Soury-Lavergne, p. 255.

on an awareness of human dignity, a source of both humility and self-esteem, this ability to discern would be seen in natural and modest behavior. The young women educated in the houses of Notre Dame were encouraged to model themselves on the Virgin Mary in their intellectual and spiritual integrity.

Consecrated to the Sacred Hearts of Jesus and Mary,[142] the Congregation of Saint Clotilde also chose the figure of Mary as a model to contemplate and imitate. The emphasis was similarly placed on the interior life, a condition needed to live and grow in union with Christ. Mary is the guide and the path:

> It is to the tabernacle of the Son of God made man that we must go in order to study the virtues of Jesus Christ, fill ourselves with his Spirit, learn to live from his life in order to say, along with Mary, these words of the apostle: "I live, no longer I, but Christ who lives in me" (Galatians 2:20).[143]

The behaviors encouraged are discretion, attention, and confidence, evoked by these words of John the Evangelist: "Do whatever he tells you." Patience within courage marks this gospel standard.

As already pointed out, the name of an Institute projects its identity. The model for living proposed by Jeanne de Lestonnac, Alix Leclerc, and Antoinette Desfontaines is unequivocally the person of Mary. Their distinctions arise from their underlying

---

142 The Society of the Sacred Heart is also consecrated to the Heart of Mary. Cf. *Constitutions de la Société du Sacré Cœur, Sommaire*, première partie, Fin et esprit de la Société, p. 139.

143 *De l'esprit de la Société*, cited in *Congrégation de Sainte-Clotilde, Règle de vie*, (extraits), p. 11, Archives.

culture, their educational goals, and their respective audience. To what specific traits, then, were the students of Lorraine called under a similar patronage?

When Decorum Pairs with Modesty

The evangelical basis of the Congregation of Notre Dame is the story of the Wedding at Cana. At the center of the event is the person of Jesus, who on this occasion begins his apostolic life. Mary is present, along with the Apostles. Discreetly, she redirects the demands that are made of her to the one who is "sent by the Father, rich in mercy." Against this referential horizon, the educational purpose is derived: "To be the first to give our human eyes, our eyes of humanity and mercy, to the suffering poor.[144] It is ultimately a question of assuring a human and a professional training that will lead to life of dignity, thereby assuring both self-esteem and the appreciation of others. An Augustinian culture, where *dilectio* and *libertas* go hand in hand, is implicit in the generosity proposed as the ideal of a life of action. The mercy of the Father is the source of the restored freedom that is.

According to this principle, the essential thing is to teach the day students "to live and live well."[145] This implies an unconditional respect for the young girl—whatever her frailties or weaknesses—in a way that will help her develop her aptitudes and prepare her for the requirements of a professional life. This

---

144 *Opuscules* du Bx P. Fourier, concernant la Congrégation de Notre Sauveur, Verdun, 1886-1889, t. II, p. 480. Quoted by P. Sagot, *L'instruction en Lorraine dans les écoles de Pierre Fourier.*

145 *Les vrayes Constitutions de la Congrégation Notre-Dame*, Troisième partie, 17-45.

type of relation requires both generous awareness and goodness that becomes patience. Because this idea of the person is derived from Augustine, the teachers encourage both aspiration and free will. A generous perspective invites the students to "rely in all confidence and without fear on their teachers." Because they feel unconditionally valued, they are meant to love their neighbor according to the gospel's message.

The moral basis of Alix Leclerc and Pierre Fourier's educational plan was to find an interior freedom, a freedom rediscovered. Its key component is self-esteem, the fruit of modesty and well-being. Much like the potter who molds the clay, the teachers attempt to "encourage them to develop the desire and firm resolution to behave with modesty."

The same recommendation can be found, expressed in similar terms, in the next-to last article of the rules for civility and well-being[146]: "The Mistresses will take particular care to instill the doctrine carefully in the spirits of their disciples, the practice, the desire and the firm resolution to persevere always in this task." These words emphasize the unique spirit of the project of the Congregation of Notre Dame's project.

The civic aspect is present from the outset in the *Preamble* to the Constitutions. To characterize the behavior of students with respect to their teachers—figures of authority—Pierre Fourier chooses familiar images: "Their respect regarding their school mistresses is the model, formula & pattern for that which they owe daily and should owe for the rest of their lives to those men & women who will be their superiors, & who govern &

---

146 Pierre Fournier, here too, shows a pioneering spirit. A full century later, in 1703, J.-B. de la Salle was to publish *The Rules of Christian Wellbeing and Civility*, used by boys from poor families.

will govern them throughout their lives."[147] In this way, they would understand reliance along with propriety. Ancillary to wellbeing, it contributed to the appreciation and awareness of girls from a "modest social background."

Another educational objective also contributed to social assimilation: to speak the language of the country correctly. This recommendation was stipulated as follows: "One will endeavor to teach them to learn to speak, & pronounce the language of the country, used by respectable persons, & the best understood: without, however, bringing to it anything of affectation or ostentation." Along with the rule of modesty, this practice reinforced the social models of the day.

Reserve and humility, moderation and self-control, goodness and gentleness thus constitute the educational principles of Pierre Fourier and Alix Leclerc. Modesty not only guided behavior and language, it also informed the student's attitude and self-image. It followed the model of respect owed to one's surroundings or to one's parents. It characterized the portrait of a young woman educated by the Religious of the Congregation of Notre Dame.

Formation according to Christian virtues is a common goal of educational monasteries. But within a given term or expression, certain characteristics or emphases are quite specific. And so it is with modesty and honesty. Was such a variation present in the educational plan of the students at the houses of the Sacred Heart? Put in other terms, what kind of living and being did this education inspire in its students?

---

147 *Les vrayes Constitutions,* p 51.

With Generosity, Beyond the Frontiers

The ideal proposed to young girls attending Sacred Heart institutions has been made apparent throughout the first part of this book. Nevertheless, a document entitled *Instructions of Father Druilhet on the Spirit of a Child of the Sacred Heart* allows us to see it anew. This manuscript, unpublished, presents us with a double interest. The first is due to its author, who contributed to the writing of the Constitutions at the request of Fathers de Clorivière and Varin. The second interest relates to its dating: the instructions were given in 1822 and 1823, that it to say at a time when the Institute was taking its definitive shape. The process for pontifical approbation was in progress; the rules and plans of study had just been codified and applied to all of the schools.

The three instructions[148] of Father Druilhet had as their objective to raise awareness of the particular vocation of a Sacred Heart student. The first, dated November 3, 1822, targets the identity of the Institute. The second, given on March 1, 1823, defines the educational style that flows from it. The third, July 30, 1823, highlights the ways in which the boarding students were to realize this ideal. The whole is clarified by an account of the Institute's founding.

From the beginning, the conversation takes on a familial tone. Imagining the arrival of new students, Julien Druilhet notes their reason for being at the Sacred Heart boarding school in Amiens. To sharpen interest, he moves into a question and answer format. And he makes this surprising remark, "Fortunately in France today, there are good and even excellent

---

148 *Instructions du R.P. Druilhet sur l'esprit d'une enfant du Sacré-Cœur*, 1822, A.G.S-C., D-I.

boarding schools where you would be taught the sciences and the virtues and where you would remain for the comfort of your parents, while at the same time sanctifying you and hoping for your salvation. If you were with the Ursuline Ladies or at one of the other pious houses destined for the teaching of youth and I were to pose this same question, you would have reason to give me this answer; it would be just, it would be good, and you would need to make me no other. But at the Sacred Heart, such an answer does not suffice. Your vocation here is sublime, and it is for an altogether different reason that you are here. God, in calling you here and in having you come here, has a goal beyond that of simply making you a good Christian." Why this elitist discourse? What can possibly be at the root of it? Why is this vocation qualified as *sublime*?

The character of the Society of the Sacred Heart is then sketched out through an origin story. With reference to the Society of the Fathers of the Sacred Heart, its goal is "to create a reflowering and rebirth of religion in the midst of our world."[149] Apostolic spirituality is defined as the knowledge of God's immense love, giving rise to gratitude and service. Next, the founding of the women's society is recalled: "These holy fathers came from France. Their first concern, once they arrived in Paris, was to realize that it would be not only useful but necessary for the advancement of their work and for the reestablishment of religion that women, inspired by the same spirit, do for young girls what they had already begun for young men. And having shared this thinking with a group of pious women already

---

[149] According to Pauline Perdrau, Madeleine Sophie Barat recognized this goal as being the very first. *Les loisirs de l'Abbaye*, Tome II, Rome, 1936, A.S-C.F., p. 13.

brimming with the same zeal as theirs, they soon came together and devoted themselves as well to the instruction of youth. This is how the Sacred Heart began."

The second instruction specifies the emblematic character of the boarding school at Amiens: "It is from this house, as from a cradle, that the Society of the Sacred Heart spread throughout the rest of France." And the third instruction notes the Society's expansion: "Since the beginning of the Society, you can count more than a thousand children of the Sacred Heart, and this number continues to grow, so that you become one body that, spreading itself throughout the world and enlivening students with the same spirit, spreads the love of the divine Heart of Jesus everywhere."

Father Druilhet skillfully highlights a vocation which understands that of the apostles: "Yes, my children, it will be by your example that you teach the world the nature of the Heart of Jesus, that you win hearts to make it loved and glorified throughout the world. This special kind of preaching, as genuine as the traditional one, is far more effective. In this way, you can announce Jesus Christ to far more people, because in our churches, we make our voices heard only to a small number of the faithful. We preach the truth for all, but most people do not come to listen."

The missionary service of the students of the Sacred Heart fits that of the founding idea. It consists of knowing the immense love of God: a characteristic gratitude and commitment accompanied by the desire to make such a love known.

This statement brings to mind the calling from the bible story, in which divine blessing accompanies the sending-out of a missionary. Here, the final object of both the blessing and the mission is the knowledge of the unfathomable and merciful love that flows from the open side of the resurrected Christ: "He had decided in his wisdom that you would be brought up in the shelter of his heart, that he would give you full knowledge of his love, that he would unveil before your eyes the admirable secrets that are enclosed there, and that for your benefit, he would open to you all the treasures of his graces and mercies." Julien Druilhet returned at each instruction to this spiritual experience, one that could catalyze a commitment; it was the focal point that determined a student's decision-making and behavior.

Such a calling eliminated any educational objectives that did not correspond to it. This conviction is affirmed often in order to create, much like a final crescendo, the profile of a student of the Sacred Heart: "It is the conformity of your heart with that of Jesus and in imitation of his virtues that people should recognize you as part of us. A child of the Sacred Heart should be a living copy of Jesus Christ and carry with her everywhere the love and the zeal by which he himself was received by men. Her desire to make this known, to love and to glorify it, should be ardent and unflagging, and she should not weary from the task until she sees the Sacred Heart honored and glorified throughout the world."[150] And so the qualification of *sublime*, accorded to this calling, arises from both the model to be followed and the missionary challenge.

The student's religious education prepares her for it, as prescribed in the Constitutions. It has a triple objective: the understanding of faith, the accomplishment of one's duties, and the propagation of the faith. Devotion to the Sacred Heart is the source of her missionary zeal. After the student's doctrinal and

---

150 *Les Instructions du R. P. Druilhet,* p. 24.

moral training, it is offered as the final goal of her education.[151] To this end, the educators should have little difficulty in "turning their young hearts, which are naturally tender and sensitive, toward the divine Heart of Jesus, and making them recognize in this lovable Heart the center and hearth of the ardent fire that burns for humanity and for them in particular."[152] The proposed meditation follows these insights: the expressions "turning their young hearts" and "making them recognize" indicate that the whole person is involved, and the entire experience leads to social commitment.

The third instruction completes the portrait of a Sacred Heart student. In view of this evangelical engagement, the virtues "that the title Child of the Sacred Heart requires are sturdy, solid, and courageous." It is also a question of modesty, zeal, and generosity. Modesty here acquires a special significance, one of humility and gentleness. Generosity refers to Christ's own behavior: "What can possibly be more generous than the Heart of Jesus? And what does this adorable heart expect from its students if not a great generosity?" To achieve this mission, the student must base her life and behavior on the model of Christ.

This account helps us to grasp the spiritual roots of the Institute and the raison d'être of the schools of the Sacred Heart. It echoes Sophie's *original idea of the little Society*, to the point that it seems almost an exact copy.

The final characteristic of the educational style of the Sacred Heart houses is the sense of belonging to a community that is both committed and active. In the face of recent societal

---

151 *Les Instructions du R. P. Druilhet*, p. 24.

152 Dominique Sadoux, Pierre Gervais, *La vie religieuse, Premières Constitutions des religieuses de la Société du Sacré-Cœur*, Beauchesne, Paris, 1986, p. 296.

obstacles—godlessness, hostility to religion, corruption, and social disturbance of every kind—a concerted action is required. To suggest it, Julien Druilhet chose the word "league," a term already used to characterize the first community of the Fathers of the Sacred Heart. He used it now to designate the two educational communities in Amiens, that of the Jesuits and that of the Religious of the Sacred Heart. The challenge was comprehensive: to combat the forces of evil, symbolized by the "beast" of the Apocalypse.[153]

The philosophy of the Enlightenment was condemned as the cause of this godlessness:

> Today, religion is no longer attacked by heresies, but many oppose its practice. Many seek to destroy it entirely. Contemporary philosophy directly attacks the religion of Jesus Christ and would like, if it could, to dethrone God himself. So it is crucial that others oppose them and do what they can to uphold the cause of God. This other is you, my dear children, and all the souls devoted to the Sacred Heart who, lined up beneath his banner, must make war, fully armed, against godlessness and uphold the glory and honor of God. But the arms that you must utilize, my children, are the virtues and the spirit of the Sacred Heart.

The tone is militant and the assertions direct: "France was at that time without God, without faith, without law, without king, without doctrine."

---

153 The critiques of Marie de Flavigny, boarding student in Paris between 1818 and 1819, are understandable in reference to such invective. Daniel Stern, *Mémoires, souvenirs and journaux de la Comtesse d'Agoult*, Mercure de France, 1940, A. S-C.F., p. 153-154.

To the children of the Sacred Heart, God would unveil and open the treasures of his grace and mercy. He would empower them to fight the godless hordes.

To judge from these remarks, belonging to a school of the Sacred Heart would establish, ipso facto, a privileged relationship with Christ and "incorporate" a student, whether she liked it or not, into the Sacred Heart "battalion." This attempt to join scholarly identity to spiritual goals suggests a simplistic use of the original symbol. What cultural elements contributed to it?

In all likelihood, it had its roots in the thinking of the Restoration,[154] shared by the preacher and many of the teachers. But a millenarian current—based on a fundamentalist reading of the Apocalypse and aligned with the idea of war against the Antichrist—might also have prompted it. Made clear in the Instructions of Father Druilhet, it can be found in the exhortations of other Jesuit priests.

In their relationships, former students were called to extend the work of their teachers because their own calling shared the same spirituality. It is thus not surprising that they were competent "auxiliaries" of the Jesuits and the Mesdames of the Sacred Heart.

As already outlined, this sense of combat engaged in for the faith was at the origin of the women's orders founded during the Counter Reformation. A similar opinion was held by some: the significant influence of a woman on her environment. Therefore, it was thus important to take great pains with her education, to give her the means that would prepare her for her future life.

---

154 A somewhat miraculous understanding of the world underlies the expression of this ecclesial concern.

Within the post-Revolutionary context, the adversary is no longer just the heretic, but first and foremost the godless revolutionary. The precise response given by the Society of the Sacred Heart applied at once to the target population, to the proposed example, and to the Sacred Heart devotion to "communicate with all nations."

The expression of these components was particular to the Institute, and the international dimension could be seen in the original plan. Girls brought up in Sacred Heart schools were all called to this work, even if the work addressed itself specifically to the boarding students, members of the ruling classes. In carrying out this work, they also benefitted from it: to live an ideally committed life, they had only to imitate Christ, the source of true "restoration." Of this Good News, each one was a messenger. Together, they were its witness.

From the Foundation to the Vatican II Council

In 1801, a boarding school was established in Amiens. A plan of studies was written in 1804. It established what the less bold plans of the Convention had not known how to establish an advanced level of instruction. In this French post-Revolutionary context, the educational genius of Sophie Barat consisted of promoting those intellectual abilities that permitted a young woman to achieve, for herself, a consciousness of her identity and dignity. In this regard, it was a mindset that operated within the values of the Enlightenment.

Following the style of her own education, Sophie Barat deliberately opted for a cultural education. In a society that was torn by ideological debate and violence, she proposed a way to live in the world in which the force for social transformation was received from the open side of the risen Christ: symbol of a gift freely given, sign of a renewal always offered.

After 1815, the growth of the Society of the Sacred Heart accelerated, reaching America in 1818.[155] However, the institute was also developing within the context of the French Restoration, which was becoming stronger between the years of 1815 and 1826—the year in which papal approbation marked an end to the founding stage of the Society of the Sacred Heart of Jesus.

If this conservative tendency guaranteed the recruitment of boarding students, it represented a backsliding in Sophie's original educational ambition. After the years of contradiction and struggle, the Constitutions and its rules named the institutional goals. And in 1820, the initial plan was confirmed. It received the status of original educational plan. Its blueprint was that of the *Ratio Studiorum,* transmitted through the educational writings of Pierre Fourier and Alix Leclerc, and integrating the goals of Jeanne de Lestonnac. Inspired by the convictions of her predecessors, Sophie Barat responded to a particular challenge.

This basic document would remain in use until 1852, when another plan of studies was written by Aimée d'Avenas. As such, it can be considered the original plan for all pedagogy in the boarding schools of the Society of the Sacred Heart of Jesus. While the charism of the Institute finds its expression in the Constitutions, the educational system finds its shape in the original plan. The two dynamics go together.

---

155 In 1865, at Sophie's death, the Institute counted 89 houses: 5 in Italy, 4 in England and Ireland, 5 in Belgium, Holland and Prussia, 44 in France, 2 in Poland, 3 in Spain, 23 in North America, and 3 in South America.

The institutional designs of the houses of the Society of the Sacred Heart were all alike: a boarding school, and a day school or an orphanage. The educational dimension took in both the vast horizons of the Humanities and the enclosed, familial character of the convent. The imposition of cloister maintained these well-defined contours until the coming of the Vatican II Council.

PART TWO

Toward the Accomplishment of the Founding Intuitions

The Vatican II Council revealed a Church truly opening itself up to the modern world and its values. Sabine de Valon, then superior general of the Society of the Sacred Heart, was an auditor at the third session. In that role, she witnessed the evolution that was propelling the Church. A complete overhaul of the Sacred Heart's educational service was part of this evolution: in 1964, conventual cloister was eliminated, and within a relatively short time, enormous changes took place.

This section's opening chapter, "The Post-Council Updating of the Original Project," traces the bold characteristics of this renewal, beginning with the Chapters of 1967 and 1970. New directions were taken; a new relationship with society developed, and a new missionary vigor called for a broadening of educational endeavors. New levels of collaboration with the laity prompted a broadening of the educational project. "When the Metaphor of the River Comes Alive" (Chapter 2) traces the move to root the Institute's founding symbol in its biblical source and in so doing distance itself from the image of Paray-le-Monial.[156] At the same time, a collective re-interpretation of the institutional goals was taking place; new Constitutions[157] were written in 1982. "The Fundamental Educational Principles of the Society of the Sacred Heart" (Chapter 3), identifies those goals. They express the work of education rooted in the Institute's spirituality.

---

156 See Translator's Note at the end of Part I, Chapter 2.

157 In accordance with the program of Pope Paul VI's *Motu Proprio* of August 6, 1966, *Ecclesiae sanctae*.

CHAPTER I

The Post-Conciliar Updating of the Original Project

A READING OF THE DOCUMENTS[158] of the Society of the Sacred Heart that were written between 1967 and 1970 reveals a groundswell that brought the Institute into a dynamic period of adaptation and creativity. *"To go towards"* was the watchword of this stage of renewed educational service. In the face of global challenges, the Institute reinterpreted the symbolism of its original goal.

"Enlarging the Educational Space" (section one) presents some of the changes that were in progress. "Contrasting Receptions of the New Orientations" (section two) identifies major advances and obstacles encountered along the way. "An Educational Project in Use in the United States of America" (section three) traces the set of objectives put forth by the U.S. provinces in light of the orientations adopted in 1970.

---

158 The body of writings used in this first chapter consists of the circular letters of María Josefa Bultó and Concepción Camacho, as well as the Chapter Documents from 1967, 1970, and 1976.

I. 1 Enlarging the Educational Space

The Special Chapter of 1967 well deserves the designation "Special Chapter" by virtue of the surprising dynamism that emerged there. All later innovations took their cue from this first formulation.

From Separation to Presence

A major difficulty was expressed in the preparatory documents: how to move from the issue of separation from the world into a state of belonging and presence to it. Resistance to abandoning traditional cloister was analyzed in these terms: "Our consecration was conceived as a separation from the world, and today this separation risks enclosing us in a life that is sheltered, regulated, artificial, and alien to the real lives of people in our times." One important result of this separation was that the language and environment of the young were barely known to their teachers. The rapid changes occurring in the contemporary world were certainly a major problem. But the essential factor was attributed to the cloister of the convent itself, which had developed into a sense of separation so internalized that it seemed impossible to abandon it. Adaptation and openness were needed throughout the Society, however, in order to serve the world better.

This question of openness was vigorously debated in reference to both the founder's thoughts and the Constitutions. Separation from life in the world, inherent in religious vows, was no longer identified with a retreat into a protected universe that favored one's personal sanctification and the Christian education of young girls. Rather, it was conceived of as a discussion of both what was close at hand and what was at a distance, a way to be open to the possibility of encountering the new. Such an idea was trailblazing. It opened a breach in the cloistered mentality and allowed for a new reference point: the Incarnation of Christ: "Our separation from the world should be considered neither as a flight from the world, nor as a protection from the dangers of the world, nor as a safeguarding of some sacred past, but rather as a 'distance' that allows us to confront the world as it is today, in the name of a world that the Incarnation would like it to become." This effort would call for much discernment.

The Missionary Framework for These Contacts

This transformation of institutional identity was not unique or isolated. The old principal of uniformity was, itself, under attack. And the relationship with the surrounding world underwent a complete reversal. It was no longer a case of "making young people come" into the convent; what mattered was to "go out to them" and to assure a presence among the world's disadvantaged. Several means were suggested: "go out and connect with those in vacation spots, get involved with literacy campaigns, in programs sponsored by the FAO; visit the neighborhoods of the poor, participate in social organizations, etc." The list, while open-ended, clearly called for education to be extended beyond the convent walls.

Through the development of new ideas for mission(encounter – unity in diversity – nearness and distance), the whole frame of reference was shaken up, shifted, modernized, fifteen years before the writing of new Constitutions. Several educational developments were already present:
- openness to political and international life;
- promotion of women's rights;

- socialization: training in interconnectedness;
- importance of science, technology and the arts.

These new directions were prompted by the Council's understanding of what it means to be a person. Such key values as dignity and solidarity, responsibility and competence, righteousness and justice, loyalty, welcome and dialogue found support.

As called for in *Gaudium et Spes*,[159] respect for the dignity of the human being was required with respect for all, "without distinctions of social class." This proposal found unanimous consent and brought with it a significant change in institutional attitudes and choices. Any pattern of social caste within the schools had to cease at once, as well as any airs of superiority or self-satisfaction. The doors were to be opened to every socio-economic level.[160]

But the elitist spirit, present from the beginning, was very much alive. How could the educators change this cultural image?

Education, a Place for Revealing the Love of Christ

The document of the 1967 Special Chapter proposed an extended educational perspective, after having laid down the basic tenets. The document's title reads:

Special Chapter
October 1 – December 14, 1967
Orientations *ad experimentum*

---

[159] *Gaudium et Spes*, Ch. 1.

[160] *Travaux préparatoires au Chapitre spécial*, 1967. Fin et esprit de la Société, A.G. S-C., I., Box 20.

The first article, "Plan of Action for the Special Chapter," sets for the objective of the assembly: "Following the example of Madeleine Sophie, who listened to the call of her times in order to found a new institute, we must:
> a) consider the needs, aspirations and values of the world of today;
> b) rethink the structures of the Society in view of these needs, in order that its service to the Church, according to its charism, be more effective.

The integrity of the new model can be seen in its inclusiveness. Its continuity lies in a statement of educational goals that depict the world and human history:

a) Introduction

Humankind is faced today with the enormous problem of *development* in all its meanings. The history of salvation is written in the heart of this ongoing evolution.

"In effect, it is a question of saving humankind; of renewing and revitalizing human society." (*Gaudium et Spes*, 3)

We must understand our "sense of mission" in this multicultural and secularized world that leads to Christ.

b) Conclusion

Humanity moves toward Christ through this evolution. The Church accompanies humanity "and experiences the same earthly lot the world does. She serves as a leaven and as a kind of soul for human society as it is to be renewed in Christ and transformed into God's family. [*Gaudium et Spes* 40-42, Translation of Latin Original by the Holy See]

Human progress and the history of salvation are interwoven like the woof and weft of the same fabric. They paint the background of the realm of education with broad strokes: playwriting with ecclesial issues.

Three actors stand on this worldwide stage: the teachers, Christ, and humanity. The crux of the plot is that "Humankind is faced today with the enormous problem of development in all its guises." Our present loss of direction is a result of a cultural breakdown; traditional reference points are no longer useful markers, and new theories seem to be running dry. From Christ—the central figure in the production—will come the dénouement. But how?

The resolution of the plot lies in an encounter and a recognition. Christ "fully discloses humankind to itself," revealing a sense of humanity and dignity to every human being. Education, then, offers a most likely setting for this revelation and for discovering the meaning of existence: "It is education that will help humanity to find itself and become capable of forging its own destiny and renewing human society."

A New Reference, the Rights of Man

Moving forward required giving priority "to the service of the human person within the Church." The chief criterion is charity. This priority was also that of Sophie Barat, but it clung to a teleological understanding of the world—within a hierarchical society where the idea of order was essential. But on this point, the 1967 Chapter Document reflected a fundamental cultural shift: the underlying ideology was no longer royalist or ultramontane, but democratic. The established criterion was no longer a hierarchical order that had to be respected at all costs, but it was replaced by the rights of the human person: "Today's world places value, with a new level of force, on the dignity of the human person, his need for justice, for authenticity, for freedom, and for love," realized through the right to life, education, and liberty.

The underlying science stands in opposition to past images of society: "The human person affirms his or her right to liberty and no longer accepts anything that would violate it. He or she assumes all the responsibilities that come with such liberty." The "virtues of risk-taking are more highly valued than those of security." The writers expressed this idea thus: "Responsible for the work of education that the Church has given us, we must offer evidence, individually and collectively, of justice, authenticity, liberty and love."[161] This vision of the world and understanding of the human person were the backdrop against which the new educational practices would be mounted. New language confirmed the goal of the Institute: "To reveal the human love of God; to center our educational service on generosity."

Daughters of the Church and Daughters of the Enlightenment
This Christocentric dimension of history and fellow feeling for persons today were wholly in keeping with the founder's thinking. As we see in the writings of Sophie Barat, the future is intentionally left open; the view of the world is positive. But the basis for this optimism is not limited to the light of reason and its capacity for innovation and unlimited adaptation to the social and natural environment. It comes from another source of light and truth: the Incarnation of the Word of God in the history of humanity.

---

161 *Travaux préparatoires*, p. 17.

From this point of view can be a new educational system, one consisting of eight criteria. The first three follow the original plan of studies. The remaining five offer new directions. Hunger and ignorance, two of society's ills are emphasized and call for serious changes in the management of institutional goods as well as development of new works.

"In a world where humanity is becoming increasingly aware of its own value, education acquires a primordial importance; it is education that allows a human to become human." From the beginning, this first criterion places education in a contemporary environment. It connects with Kant's understanding that the idea of humanity determines the work of education. To be aware of the dignity of the human being and recognize his or her role within the world, that was the goal of the original plan of the Society of the Sacred Heart. For Sophie Barat, this idea came from a source other than the Enlightenment: "In this pluralist, secularized world that journeys toward Christ, we realize more and more the value of the human person. It is toward this light that we must direct the renewal and adaptation of our educational work."

The "first educational goal" of the original plan, religion, is set forth in the second criterion. It originates in a person-centered culture modeled on relationships: "In a world where interpersonal relations assume a growing value, one of education's first tasks is to render human beings capable of dialogue." The educational plan of 1804, whose goal was to enable students to speak and write with ease and grace, was rephrased. Now it adopted a spiritual goal: to prepare future witnesses to Christ for "a world where atheism continues to grow." The approach was meant to be experiential. The warning against a philosophical approach was clear: "Faith is not a defense against error, nor simply an intellectual assent to a truth that our teaching might highlight. Faith is a way of life, a response of one's entire being to the Holy Trinity." In addition, "It is up to us, the teachers, to prepare the terrain for this encounter." The wording is new. The goal of *the primordial idea of the little Society* is translated into language accessible to all, by means of the "encounter."

New Vectors, Dialogue, and Collaboration

- to give our students the kind of education that will prepare them for their future role.
- to emphasize, whenever possible, advanced studies: this is part of the patrimony that our Holy Mother bequeathed to us.
- to pay more attention to the needs of our teachers' college and university students.

One principal idea stands out: God desires the continuing evolution of humanity.[162] This notion brings together "participating in progress" with "being an apostle of Christ."

Another link with the contemporary milieus clearly seen in criteria 4 and 5. The connection is expressed through collaboration, interreligious dialogue, and multiculturalism. Such collaboration involves both old and new partners: other scholarly institutions and pastoral leaders. The keynote is to "depart from a certain isolationism in order to think about the

---

162 The influence of Teilhard de Chardin's evolutionist perspective is evident here. This perspective attempts to resolve a major contemporary challenge as follows: "Scientific and technological progress are all part of a continuous movement of evolution desired by God."

Church." This opening to ecumenical dialogue is significant. It is light years away from the earlier restrictions with respect to other Christian denominations. The prevailing attitude toward other cultures was also changed. If Sophie Barat recommended adapting to "the customs of the country," such adaptation nevertheless invoked a kind of ethnocentrism that was reinforced by the uniform practices within the schools. The desire to do away with such uniformity was clearly articulated here. It was recommended *not* to impose on young nations—proud of their recent independence—a foreign culture.

A Demand for Justice Linked to Love

The appreciation of cultural and religious differences was accompanied by a reworking of the educational goal: "To develop a social awareness within our students that demands a lived Christianity." This new expression of the social objective brought with it a level of questioning, found in Criterion 6: "In a world where hunger and ignorance must be combated by means of education, we must ask ourselves:

- if our students leave us with a realistic sense of social justice and the determination to work to change the world;
- if we ourselves are educating those students who have the most need of us. In order to regroup our forces and go toward those who are disadvantaged, we must suppress those works that have outlived themselves, at times even those that are in full activity but less necessary, in order to create centers of education in the poorer areas, or in the small towns where the need for a Christian education is sorely felt."

Students deprived of their basic rights can be heard in these words.[163] It was these scourges of modern and "enlightened" society that the Institute decided to address head-on in order to oppose them. Such an option was considered "a requirement of justice and love," and it brought with it a call to participate. To accomplish this, a creative strategy was developed. It took its cue from the directions expressed in Paul VI's encyclical *Populorum Progressio*.[164]

From this time forward, the educational goal of Sacred Heart education consisted in training students to "a realistic sense of social justice and a determination to work to change the world."[165] This was in keeping with the spirit of the original plan, but its innovation arose from the conviction that came with it and the international context that required it. In effect, "arrived at this point in the history of the world, where 35 million of our brothers and sisters die each year of hunger and misery, divesting ourselves of the goods not required for our apostolate, as well as sharing—in the spirit of brotherhood—those which our apostolate obliges us to possess, has become a requirement of justice and love." This testament brought together the concepts of justice and love for one's fellow beings afflicted by the current disasters. It established a decision-making process the outline

---

163 Sensitivity to these global problems was part of a larger ecclesial current: the Catholic Committee against Hunger was created on May 25, 1961; in March 1966, it became the Committee against Hunger and for Development; in 1967, the French bishops founded the Catholic Delegation for Cooperation.

164 Paul VI, *Populorum Progressio* (23).

165 In 1965, an association was created: AMASC (*Association Mondiale des Anciennes Élèves du Sacré-Cœur*, or World Association of Sacred Heart Alumnae). Its purpose was to cooperate in an effective way with the educational tasks of the Society of the Sacred Heart.

of which might be expressed as follows: This driving force of justice and sharing, founded on the concept of brotherly love, brings to mind "reparation," which is intimately connected to the devotion to the Sacred Heart. Might it be possible that a translation of the "primordial idea" of the Institute is already under way?

A plan was set forth in Criteria 7 and 8, following a forward-looking expression of openness. Below is the list articulated in Criterion 7:

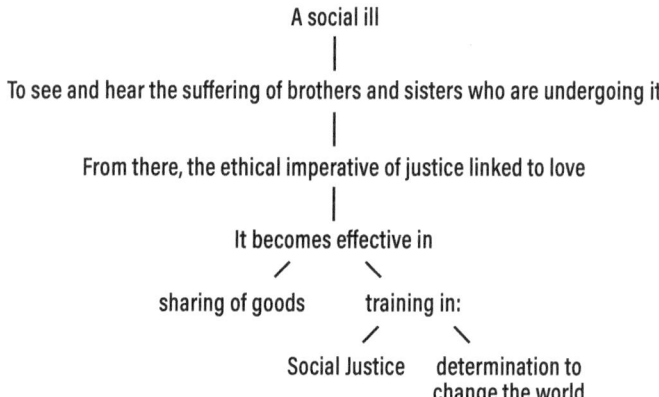

"In addition to our educational institutes, primary and secondary schools, normal schools, university colleges, other means are in our power today: teaching in the parishes, in the inner city, catechetical centers, student centers, classes in adult education, centers for the handicapped and the abandoned, visits to families according to apostolic needs, vacation camps, participation in missionary teams; finally, every work of education as the need arises."[166]

---

166 Society of the Sacred Heart, Special Chapter, 1967, Part Six, Apostolic Life, p. 64.

The criteria for making one's choices were made clear:
- better service,
- greater urgency,
- more global well-being,
- an enlightened outlook.

Criterion 8 includes an unprecedented feature. It deliberately includes educational interventions outside the boundaries of the ecclesial world, within "universities, secondary schools, etc." With the clear intention to broaden the scope of practices and areas of involvement, the openness is at its fullest: "We must always maintain the genuine witness of our religious life. We should sow the seed of the Gospel in a secular milieu. We must read the signs of the times—they will not be the same for all countries. May we be ready, without vain regret, to live Christ in a world with new structures." The conclusion brings with it a final confirmation: "An immense field lies open before us." And as the hallmark of the institution, it brings together its guiding principles: "We must be open to progress, and create the climate of love and freedom in which each one will realize her Christian and human potentialities. . . . we shall serve the world that God has so loved."

Cloister—bound to a conventual lifestyle and formerly imposed by canon law—fell away in order to allow a major new development. "Returning to the sources of the Institute," leaving behind the issue of separation from the world for that of belonging in and presence to it, the Society of the Sacred Heart was ready to engage in new kinds of educational works, "wherever the need makes itself most fully felt." Out of all of this, the field of education emerged transformed.

I.2 Differing Receptions of the New Orientations

In order to establish a religious order of women that followed an Ignatian structure, Joseph Varin and Sophie Barat encountered obstacles arising largely from canon law. 150 years later, however, the obstacles came from within, in the sense that they emerged from institutional perceptions connected with the order's spiritual and social purposes. Some of this resistance was shared by former students who could find in the new orientations neither the scholarly tradition of old nor the language of devotion to the Sacred Heart to which they were accustomed. Many of the Religious were aware of the problem, but concern for remaining faithful to the founding charism relegated all other worries to the background. Herein lay major problems that restrained full dialogue until 1981.

Evoking a Figure: Philippine Duchesne

In her first letter,[167] written after the governmental crisis of 1967 that ended the generalate of Sabine de Valon, María Josefa Bultó named the goal that would be likely to win over the whole institute: fidelity to Sophie's original plan. In order to accomplish this, she refused to become ensnared in a doctrinal quagmire: "For some time past, many of you have been asking me to address a letter to the whole Society.... Our late Mothers General, in magnificent Circulars, have left us a wealth of spirituality on which we can always draw.... It is my wish, [however], if our

---

167 These circular letters are published in a trilingual collection—Spanish-French-English—entitled *Circular Letters of Mother María Josefa Bultó, RSCJ. Superior General of the Society of the Sacred Heart of Jesus from 1967 to 1970*. Tipografia Poliglotta della Università Gregoriana, Rome, 1991.

Lord so wills, to carry on the tradition of the Society by writing very simple letters."[168] In fact, letters 5, 7 and 9 form a triptych which, taken together, express a clear spiritual oneness.

The fifth circular[169] is addressed to American RSCJ on the occasion of the 150th anniversary of Philippine Duchesne's arrival in Louisiana. The image offered is that of a pioneer whose two central traits were discernment and missionary daring. Her strongly worded statement called for discernment in the style of an Ignatian dialogue: "Faced as you are with so many needs, such different needs... a multitude calls..., ask Him, 'Who is my neighbor? To whom can our communities in America best devote themselves?' He will show you!" The fearless character of the first missionaries mirrored their courage founded on faith in Christ.

By referring to Philippine Duchesne, Maria-Josefa Bultó transformed the traditional understanding of *mission*. She positioned the sphere of mission not "elsewhere," but here in the many details of one's local, particular surroundings. "To go to the end of the world" suddenly seemed a nearby destination, whoever the person and whatever the environment. "So go, be a neighbor!... wherever he calls you. Be a neighbor all the time, to your sisters in the community, to the student in the classroom, to the colored in the ghetto. Be a neighbor to Christ in all His poor, His needy ones, His loved ones." In this was her genius: to anchor renewal in the energy of the Society's beginnings in order to allow backward-looking images to fade away. And all of this was accomplished not through arguments set in concrete,

---

168 Letter 7, September 28 1968, p. 77.
169 Letter 5, May 1968, p. 73-75.

but through metaphors that invoked the imagination. The missionary challenge was conceived as one of nearness and distance. Calling for a great deal of trust, the superior general sent the American RSCJ out "toward all men and women—the uneducated, the poor, those who suffer."

In the aftermath of the 1967 Chapter, two educational directions were put forward: to develop within students an awareness of social justice grounded in the spirit of the Gospel and to serve the needs of the marginalized. The socio-political stakes were identified: "Your country is now a prosperous one with technical and social advantages of which Blessed Philippine would never have dreamt. You are conscious that this development in wealth and power imposes on you grave responsibilities in the field of social justice, of freedom, of peace. You are seeking ways of being a neighbor, of fighting against poverty, loneliness, hate, knowing full well that any undertaking must be gospel-inspired."

The educational purpose of the Institute was reaffirmed: "Each one of our students should leave us with this anxiety for social justice, this determination to make this world a better place, in an evangelical spirit, in fraternal love." Such an education was not reserved for just a few or for some elite group. This idea needed to characterize Sacred Heart education, including the way budgets were managed. "Will you allow me to quote our Blessed Philippine on this subject? . . . She wrote, 'for our large houses in Louisiana such a small offering would provide for the simple needs of our poor Indians, and for them it would mean only a little less beauty.'"

María Josefa Bultó appended this goal: "To love God and humankind with the love of the pierced Heart of God made man." As in the document of 1967, the broad perspective of the

Incarnation was given as the backdrop for education. The figure of Philippine thus stepped aside to reveal the only model to imitate: Christ. At the same time, the missionary opportunities of 1967 were firmly anchored in the founding spirit. With a brilliant stroke, a path was opened up: to work for justice, liberty and peace.

When the Model Shatters the Image

One year later, another circular letter again referred to this pioneer. The challenge had not diminished. Some members found themselves in a double bind: focused on a bygone past, on the one hand, and impatient to move forward on the other.[170] Underlining the importance of visiting different provinces, María Josefa Bultó recalled "the stunning relevance of the message of Mother Duchesne." Taking Philippine as an example, she focused on the missionary desire that united her to Mother Barat: "To make known the love of the Heart of Christ at all costs." Writing with great skill, she linked their two vocations. Philippine could be seen as the overseas co-founder, recognizing that Madeleine Sophie was unable to take on this role herself because of her many responsibilities.

By recalling the era of foundations in "new lands," toward unknown territory, Maria-Josefa Bultó proposed Philippine as model for all religious of the Sacred Heart during this period of change. To take her as an example shattered the traditional, conventual prototype in which uniformity stood for of unity. The image of Philippine, "the woman with a heart of oak, the woman who is always praying, the woman who wore herself out

---

170 M-J. Bultó, Circular Letter of June 29, 1969, p. 81-84.

to be the neighbor of others," served as a figurehead. She cut through erroneous notions of fidelity and through her ability to bring others along with her, created a collaborative renewal. Her exceptional way of being was suggested as a model for all to adopt in order to resolve conflicting positions, troublesome disagreements, and divisive misunderstandings.

A single mission unified a range of activities and commitments. By taking these steps, María Josefa Bultó led the institute out of the past into the present, to a world marked by variety, involvement, and shared responsibility.

When Departure is Rebirth

This departure was a beginning, as suggested by the metaphor of a renaissance[171] that is found throughout the seventh circular letter.[172] The superior general expressed a sense of *aggiornamento*[173]: "to be reborn in the way we love Christ." And she emphasized the conditions under which such an enterprise could be realized: "We shall draw fraternal love from the open Heart of Christ, for the shortest way, the only way we can learn to love one another truly, courageously, is to abide in the living Christ." In no uncertain terms, she named the chief component of renewal: how to be in relationship.

María Josefa Bultó highlighted a family trait: the strength that comes from loving and that requires us to "constantly

---

171 The appearance of the biblical metaphor of the river within the congregational culture was preceded by that of the renaissance. One might argue that the transformation initially took place at the level of the collective imagination.

172 7th Circular Letter of M.-J. Bultó, dated September 28, 1968, p. 44-45.

173 Tr. Note: This term, meaning *modernization* or *bringing up to date*, was one frequently used during Vatican II.

put on" the humility and meekness of Christ. The underlying Pauline metaphor calls to mind an evangelical struggle. The proposed interiority, a component of an institutional ethic, had nothing to do with intimacy. Rather, it called for "that patience of love which is the mark of the truly strong."

The following description pointed to the source of this wisdom: "Only hearts that are meek and humble, converted by the meek and humble Master, can hold this strong love."[174] This statement brings to mind the figure of the servant in the second part of the Book of Isaiah—a servant who is not recognized because he does not appear in the fullness of his strength. This image recurs in the ninth letter, accompanied by the idea of Christ's kenosis, a basic theme of the Incarnation. These depictions of the self-emptying of the Son of God offered a necessary direction in this time of renewal. The challenge of that time was to "be reborn in our way of loving the Lord."

This metaphor, however, had been used by Philippine Duchesne from the time when she served as Secretary General. The *Journal of the General Council of 1815*, the event that resulted in the adoption of the Constitutions, relates the following: "December 16, 1815, was the time of the rebirth, or rather of the self-identification, of our Society, which had always wanted to be glorified by belonging in both name and practice to the Sacred Heart of Jesus."[175] The verbs *to be reborn* and *to affirm* are seen as intimately linked with the Institute's naming.

---

174 The imitation of Christ is the theme of the *Devotio Moderna* [Tr. note: a religious movement of the fourteenth to sixteenth centuries that focused on meditation and the interior life]. To unite ourselves with the "dispositions of Christ" is a New Testament theme by which the spirituality of the Heart of Christ is nourished within us.

175 Adèle Cahier, *Vie de la vénérable Mère Barat*, A. S-C.F., p. 240.

The parallels between these two documents, written 150 years apart, are significant. It was a question of a family treasure being brought up to date. This inheritance, it must be recalled, did not belong to the teachers alone. It applied to everyone involved in the work of education, because the rebirth brought together a way of life and a plan of action for the entire organization. At risk was the educational character of the institute, whose fundamental purpose the 5th Circular Letter had made explicit: a struggle that would bring about greater justice, fraternity, and peace.

This direction took shape in letters 10 to 20, where María Josefa Bultó described the application of the 1967 Chapter orientations and the preparations for Chapter of 1970. Requesting the collaboration of all, she invited her sisters to adopt a new kind of missionary life. Uniformity and centralization gave way to plurality, participation, and subsidiarity. The mission became the single unifying element within the international community. A courageous pathway from old ways to new values had been set forth.

A Great Cry, That of the Poor

The phrase "A great cry, that of the poor" had a major impact on the preparatory documents for the Chapter of 1970. "The Latin American bishops cannot remain indifferent before the immense social injustices that exist in Latin America and that keep the majority of its people in a pitiful poverty, one too often close to inhuman misery. A profound cry can be heard springing from the millions of human beings who ask their pastors for a liberation that will not come out of the blue."[176] Its impact, which was international, profoundly affected the Society of the Sacred Heart. "The call of the poor has been heard and asks that our response take the shape of concrete action."

One decision was cast in a new way: "to go into those places and to those people who are the most abandoned—there where others do not go, or cannot go, or do not wish to go." Framed in this way, the decision proposed unprecedented openness: no longer based on cloister, it flowed from the particular work of the institute (to reveal the Love of Christ through education), which was understood to be "the integral development of the human being for his or her liberation in Jesus Christ."

This idea brought together a new interpretation of the purpose of the institute with an outline of the means of carrying it out. Fundamental educational goals were already highlighted: to train young people to be aware of injustices and the structures of oppression, and capable of transforming society in light of the Gospel.

It also envisioned another outlook, no less courageous: daring to undertake in the interim an evaluation of the existing institutions. This would involve several measures: evaluation, strategic planning, and data. Such evaluation would examine every partnership and educational community. Such endeavors as inter-religious dialogue and ecumenism were approved. Integration of religious into a wider sphere was encouraged. Each province was asked to find concrete forms of service, adapted

---

176 *L'Eglise dans la transformation actuelle de l'Amérique latine, Conclusions de Medellin, La pauvreté de l'Eglise,* Paris, Cerf, 1992, Quoted by Olivier Compagnon in *Histoire du christianisme des origines à nos jours,* sous la direction de J-M. Mayeur, *tome XIII, Troisième partie, Chap. IV,* Desclée, Paris, 2000, p. 538.

to its location and the social circumstances of its country. Every religious, wherever she worked, was asked to take on an unwaveringly positive attitude toward the poor.

Participation was meant to operate, the point being to "create opportunities for dialogue at every level." The skills needed were enumerated: "a sufficient sense of human value; a regard for interpersonal relationships; a theological and pastoral formation that permits one to encounter other ideologies and accomplish a meaningful task of evangelization; a social and cultural formation; a professional competency, and even a specialization, necessary for rendering a valuable service in today's world." These were the goals of training, and they are in practice today.

When Contrary Winds Blow

Nevertheless, in the course of establishing this new institutional identity, one obstacle became increasingly evident. For a century and a half, the institute's social identity had been that of a teaching order. The education offered in its schools had determined its public face. And in certain minds, especially those of some parents or former students, "ends" and "means" had been conflated. At the General Council of 1820, Father Varin had identified this very confusion: "If you believe that the first goal of your Society is the education of youth, you are wrong; it is, rather, the adoration of the Heart of Jesus." Even if these intentions were alive in the institutional memory, representations of them had become confused and characterized by misunderstandings and argument. The changes being undertaken were often felt to be too quick—even incomprehensible.

And a kind of disorientation came over those who tended to identify the educational mission with the scholastic institution.

A combination of social factors contributed to this situation: the decline of traditional humanism, the emergence of globalization, a perceived crisis within civilization and, in Europe, within the educational system. Administrative constraints imposed by state or higher education authorities conflicted with the traditional educational priorities of the Institute. The status of private education varied widely from country to country. The validity of certain schools was periodically questioned. From there emerged a profound questioning filled with apprehension: Was abandoning the boarding school model and opting for other forms of education not to abandon the original plan of the founder and—in this way—to lose the Institute's identity?

As preparations for the 1976 General Chapter were under way, a range of opinions brought these concerns to the surface: "Depending on the circumstances in which they find themselves, certain Religious find our schools to be indispensable; others believe that we should be engaged in education—but not necessarily doing so in schools that belong to us; still others question the value of our schools, which they see not as instruments of liberation, but as institutions that prepare students to enter into an unjust system—or at worst educate an elite that might subsequently become the oppressor."[177] Such conflicting points of view clashed with one another and brought about deep oppositions. Resistance and misunderstanding reinforced them.

---

177 *Réflexions de la Commission sur la Mission éducatrice*, 1976, A.G.S-C, C-I, C-4, p. 5.

In addition, the plan to develop new provisions of canon law for religious Institutes had become the goal of conservative commentators who equated "transforming institutional works" with "making institutional identity disappear."[178] This threat resulted in sowing suspicion and increasing conflict. According to some members or likeminded groups, the challenge was to safeguard the characteristic work of the Society of the Sacred Heart. Why this backlash?

As Mary Quinlan once remarked, "Because of cloister, collaboration with other religious orders and the laity had been quite limited. In many places, the sense of even belonging to a diocese had worn away. The religious moved from one house to another. Psychologically, she identified herself with the Society of the Sacred Heart."[179] Working the boarding schools had provided a kind of social standing with which many teachers identified.

The same problems confronted rewriting the Constitutions.[180] The superior general warned against relativist or fundamentalist readings that would obscure their meaning.[181] The first danger consisted of "taking those much-loved words and making them say something for today which they did not say." This

---

[178] "It is the apostolic work that establishes the distinctions between and among the various Institutes. If they abandon their proper works, they will lose their identity or their intrinsic character. This is what happens in times like these, in particular within those Institutes that undertake excessive changes." Commentary cited by M-T Virnot, RSCJ, A.S-C.F.

[179] Mary Quinlan, *Ministères de la Société du Sacré Cœur en dehors de ses écoles*, 1975, A.G. S-C., C-I, p. 1.

[180] This occurred in 1981, during preparations for rewriting the Constitutions of 1815.

[181] Letter 40, February 11, 1981, p. 100.

is caused "by taking them [the words] out of context—that is, manipulating them—however unconsciously." The second kind of reading amounts to "taking them merely literally," using the Constitutions "as a braking force, through fear of the demands which our contemporary world makes of us." Both of these approaches sidestepped a correct interpretation of the document by circumventing it or by denying its otherness. They resisted any openness to real progress. The founding document was not recognized for what it was: one capable of renewing life.

These differences of opinion in the face of the new orientations were particularly obvious upon the appearance of the 1970 Chapter document. Six months later, Concepción Camacho had to acknowledge: "The five options are simply the expression of our union and conformity to the Heart of Jesus. The close bond between the options and our end is clear for those who lived the Chapter of 1970, but many in the Society have not had this experience, and we have noted on this point, many questions asking of us a clarification on the 'vision of today,' on 'our spirituality, its characteristics, its requirements.'"[182]

The collective imagination had become blurred. While uniformity had always been reassuring, difference and diversification gave rise to anxiety and tensions.

Moreover, an individualism was changing some people's behavior; a kind of gentrification was modifying lifestyles. A shared direction was being hidden by a too easy compromise with worldly values or by impatience with a bygone past. Would another difficulty arise out of the language being used?

---

182 Letter 10, July 3, 1972, p. 20.

Solidarity "from Within"
In the documents, these Five Options appear as a declaration with five key components: internationality; educational mission; solidarity with the poor; solidarity with the Third World; renewal of the fraternal community.

In the past, the literary style used within the congregation was that of analysis, argument, and persuasion. It arose from a form of linear thinking. However, the Five Options were introduced in language that was unified and forward-looking, incorporating momentum of an ongoing evangelical call. The results were unexpected: those who depended on a traditional set of ideas found the document baffling. Its thinking—fundamental and interdependent—belonged to a culture that was foreign to them and defied comprehension.

In addition, if the document were to be seen as based on an absolute truth, the idea of unity within a pluralist approach risked being obscured. This problem was recognized in 1972: "Distinctions are being made between and among those who follow the option for the poor—these are the most advanced; those who live in the schools—these are the backward ones; and those who are in favor a community of life—those have utterly lost the sense of the mission. Such distinctions are being made as if there were five paths among which we must choose only that one which would best stimulate the sense of renewal."[183] This reasoning suggested an undermining bias. The old problem, from the days when uniformity reigned, was still active, whether as a bulwark against change or as a validation of a single model for institutional action.

---

183 C. Camacho, *Recueil de conférences*, Assemblées des provinciales, novembre 1972, Tipografia Poliglotta della Università Gregoriana, Rome, 1992, p. 14.

In the Second Option, the Society of the Sacred Heart committed itself "to meet the needs of men crushed by a life of subjection and ignorance, and above all, those of young people searching for the meaning of life."[184] This statement touched on the continuity of the work of education and confirmed harmony among the five courses of action. Fraternal sharing and consensus are the warp and weft of the document, integrating the five elements. The work of education is modified by the cultures or countries served.

The interchange between the particular and the universal created a fertile tension from which older ideas could be transformed. In effect, unity within diversity seemed to flow directly from the interaction between the charism of "union and conformity with the Heart of Christ" and the contemporary world. The term *reparation*, from the language of tradition, seemed to become *liberation*. Would this interpretation make the document airtight?

The Third Option expresses, also in new language, the institutional identity: "In light of the Gospel and of contemporary society, we wish to affirm our solidarity with the poor." The overview of the five options comes together here. It follows the pattern of humility of Christ the servant: "Christ who emptied himself and gave his life to set us free has made us his own, thus we too are committed to this work of liberation." This was the declaration of the institution as a whole. The concept of liberation would from now on characterize the work of education. The charism of the congregation would be expressed in a new way: "No matter where we are, this solidarity will mark our life." Union with Christ was the source.

---

184 Camacho, *Recueil de conférences,* Second Option, p. 14.

The ethical implications were listed next. Such oneness of thinking swept away or changed attitudes with a view toward appreciation of other cultures and traditions. It moved away from "any attitude of power and paternalism." It involved "serious work, readiness, and discipline." By its statement of plans for coordinated efforts for the Institution, the Fourth Option took an idealistic position by "confronting the dehumanizing structures of a consumer society; working toward a better distribution of the goods of this world; and organizing works from a global perspective, according to needs and the possibilities."[185]

The Third Option of the 1970 General Chapter began the updating of some components of the Institute's symbols. At the center was a charism of union and oneness with the Heart of Christ that would provide better service to the Church and the contemporary world. Here, "belonging in name and in deed" to a Christ of meekness and humility could become real. Its framework was marked by austerity and the sharing of goods, a respect for differences, and an acceptance of plurality. Liberation would be the goal for works undertaken.

I.3 An Educational Program Introduced in the United States of America

In the years following the 1970 General Chapter, the United States of America Provinces drew up a statement of educational philosophy that was to be implemented throughout the country, and whose point of departure was the new orientations. The document gives a concise and carefully planned version of

---

185 Camacho, *Recueil de conférences*, Fourth Option, p. 17.

the Five Options. It is entitled the *Goals and Criteria*, and its Preamble clearly states its purpose and its audience.

Contemporary Distinctiveness of the Schools of the Sacred Heart

The opening sentence of the Preamble highlights the fact that the Schools of the Sacred Heart in the United States are "members of a world-wide network." The current challenge follows: "As [the schools] become increasingly diverse, it becomes increasingly necessary to respond to the question: 'What makes a Sacred Heart school?' Independent but never isolated, every Sacred Heart school needs to feel the strength of belonging to a larger whole, of sharing principles and values, broad purposes, hopes and ambitions." The object of the document is to demonstrate this identity.

The program follows from its educational tradition; the grounds for the case are set forth. For the previous ten years, decentralized decision-making, increased collaboration with the laity, and the adaptation of programs and methods suited to the needs of each school have made this program necessary: "Values taken for granted or left unarticulated can become inoperative." The challenge was to articulate and transmit those educational principles that were critical to an international network of Sacred Heart schools.

These unique characteristics are spelled out as follows: "It is of the essence of a Sacred Heart school that it be deeply concerned for each student's total development: spiritual, intellectual, emotional, and physical. It is of the essence of a Sacred Heart school that it emphasize serious study, that it develop in its students social responsibility, and that it lay the

foundations of a strong faith."[186] This concept is then expressed in five educational goals:
1. Faith which is relevant in a secularized world.
2. A deep respect for intellectual values.
3. A social awareness which impels to action.
4. The building of community as a Christian value.
5. Personal growth in an atmosphere of wise freedom.

"The first three goals are taken directly from the section on education in the documents of the Society's 1970 General Chapter."[187] The expression of educational purpose is succinct and precise. The Criteria that accompany each Goal serve as a means of evaluating the project. They are "signs which indicate that the Goal is being effectively pursued." They are useful in allowing "each school, and the network as a whole to benefit fully from this process."

Let us consider them now.

The Goals and Criteria[188]

In the same way that a seal was engraved on the pediment of a

---

186 The necessity of an integral formation is reaffirmed in the exact center of the Preamble: "Whatever the orientation given to studies may be, there must be no forgetting that it involves the formation of the whole woman with a view to her own vocation within the circumstances and the times in which she lives."

187 "We envision the development of a faith capable of sustaining itself in a secularized world, a deep respect for values of the intellect, and an education with a social purpose that inspires to action."

188 The original articulation of the Goals and Criteria was published in 1975. Subsequently, the criteria were revised in 1990, 2005, and most recently in 2020. See *Goals and Criteria Sacred Heart Schools United States and Canada*, USC Province, 2020.

Sacred Heart school to indicate its identity, Goal I broadened the areas of education by characterizing it. A central belief expressed it: that the love of Christ is the foundation of the educational institution. It follows one model— that of the relationship between Christ and humanity, understood through the concepts of "meaning," "hope," "relationship, "Christ-centered institution," and "evolving tradition of the Church." The language indicates membership or belonging.

Goal I
Faith which is relevant in a secularized world
Criteria for Goal I:
1. The school recognizes its life force in the love of Jesus Christ by supporting in concrete ways the value of reflection and of prayer.
2. The total educational program affirms the belief that there is meaning in life and thereby fosters within the school community a sense of hope.
3. The religious studies program probes the relationship of God to man and to the world.
4. The school provides education to decision-making in the light of Christian principles.
5. The school presents itself to the wider community as a Christ-centered institution within the evolving tradition of the Church.

The first criterion underlines the need for training in theology and prayer, critical aspects of the Sacred Heart tradition. The second expresses the organizing principle of the educational program. The third recalls the wording of the Religious Studies program of 1805. The fourth underlines, in unequivocal terms, the Ignatian heritage. It translates, on the decision-making level, one of the objectives of the original plan: "to form women of judgment."

The first criterion of Goal Two is anchored in the educational tradition of the Institute. We hear, almost as an echo, the introductory words of the 1852 Plan of Studies, written by Aimée d'Avenas: "In order to settle on this plan, we consulted experience, and, without disdaining the older methods, without rejecting newer ones, we asked each other which ones seemed most to favor the development of the intellect." In these words can be found the groundbreaking nature of the Plan of Studies in use at the Amiens school. The same holds true today for the American schools of the Sacred Heart. Two familiar elements stand out: the importance placed on the development of "taste," i.e., to the aesthetic sense and the creative use of the imagination.

Goal II
A Deep Respect for Intellectual Values
Criteria

1. The course of study is intellectually challenging.
2. Serious study and a love of learning are encouraged.
3. Program development is based on research and evaluation.
4. Teaching/learning styles promote the development of persons who are knowledgeable, questioning, thoughtful and integrated.
5. Opportunities are provided for experiential education, which includes the element of reflection.
6. The curriculum encourages the development of aesthetic values and the creative use of the imagination.

A dynamic method remains in force, as the fifth Criterion makes explicit.[189] But there are variations in the way it is carried out. "The program is based on research and evaluation" in which the student is the main participant. The same meaning appears in Goal Three, where the accent is on training in moral and political theology with a view toward commitment.

Skill is acquired not only through reflection, but also by means of short-term commitment with other institutions and groups. The role of women has clearly changed.

Goal III
A Social Awareness that Impels to Action
Criteria

1. The school awakens a critical sense, which leads to reflection on our society and its values.
2. The curriculum includes study of the problems of the world community.
3. The school provides the knowledge and skills needed for effective action on the problems of oppression and injustice.
4. The school has programs which enable students to become actively involved in the wider community.

Awakening a critical sense is a new educational goal. The same is true for its corollary, to create an awareness of "the problems of oppression and injustice." Feminine activity is no longer limited to the domestic sphere; it reaches into the political domain. The object of reflection, "society and its values,"

---

189 It reappears in the fourth criterion of Goal Five, where self-discipline is integrated into the application of the goals.

has as its background the challenges presented by a growing globalization. Within this context, the scourge to be fought against is "oppression and injustice."

The consistency among the first three goals is clear. Christian formation takes on the orientation of the special Chapter of 1967,[190] reaffirmed in 1970[191]: "We aspire to the development of a faith capable of sustaining itself in a secularized world, to a serious esteem for intellectual values, and to educating students to a social awareness that impels to action." Their concise formulation highlights the unity of the three criteria: faith, ethics, and commitment, avoiding any drift towards abstraction. The statement is rooted not in socio-political reflection, but in "the love of Christ." The educational institution recognizes this fact and affirms it with conviction and hope. Goal Three names the atrocities that humanity is experiencing: "oppression and injustice." It provides core belief: "Union and conformity with the Heart of Christ" suggests solidarity with all those who "endure poverty and oppression."

---

190 The cry of "35 million brothers," suffering from the scourges of hunger and misery, Société du Sacré-Cœur *Chapitre spécial*, 1967, p. 57.

191 "It is the very love of Christ that forces us to respond to the needs of every person oppressed by ignorance and servitude, and above all to those of youth who seek meaning in their lives. Facing the future, we are responsible to live this mission with creativity," Camacho, *Recueil de conferences,* Second Option, p. 13.

Goal IV
The Building of Community as a Christian Value
Criteria

1. Skills needed to build community are taught and opportunities to exercise those skills are provided.
2. School policies and practices are established and reviewed in the light of Christian principles.
3. The school provides experiences of diversity, which are designed to develop an understanding and appreciation of various races, religions and cultures.
4. An effective financial aid program supports socio-economic diversity.
5. The life of the school community is deepened by an understanding of the purposes and evolving tradition of Sacred Heart education.
6. The school participates actively in the national and international network of Sacred Heart schools.
7. The program is designed to help students take their place as responsible citizens in an interdependent world.

Goal Four is implied in Goal One, and we might doubt its necessity were it not for its criteria, which reveal the reasons for its inclusion. They are organized around two essential goals: development of the capacity for relationships[192] and learning to be open to what is both broader and other than oneself.

---

192 The special Chapter of 1967 explained it in these words: "In a world where interpersonal relations assume a growing importance, one of the first roles of education is to render human beings capable of dialogue. A human being is not fully himself or herself unless in dialogue with others." But in addition and above all, this relational ability opens the way to "dialogue with God within faith." Camacho, *Recueil de conférences*, p. 54.

Historically, the education of young girls in Sacred Heart boarding schools had meant living on the campus. There, students lived in a controlled environment, monitored at all times. Goal IV provides a good example of how the founding educational principles were now reinterpreted: the building of a strong character results from collaborative action. The description of "a school of the Sacred Heart in the 1960s" demonstrates how to make that happen. Learning how to relate to others in community no longer relies on nineteenth century teaching methods but the same educational objective is at work.

The educational community becomes a laboratory wherein a Christian community is built. The goals draw on reflection and ethical behavior. It is important to foresee the process that will foster "an understanding and appreciation of various races, religions and cultures." The introduction to the social sciences in the Program of Exercises of 1805 finds here its modern translation. The positions advocated are drawn from the statements of the Chapters of 1967 and 1970. One of them, sharing, is prioritized in several different ways. The overriding purpose is to prepare students to "take their place as responsible citizens in an interdependent world."

The necessary skills are developed "by means of appropriate experiences." These last are not spelled out, for it is the responsibility of each school to adapt them to its own student population. The last paragraph of the Preamble reads: "The Goals and Criteria are *sine que non* for every school that belongs to the Sacred Heart network. They provide the framework within which each school is to develop specific Objectives appropriate to its local situation." The same holds true for learning about diversity.

The student has a shared responsibility for developing these relationships. For that, these approaches are recommended:
- an acknowledgment of others through the interest that one takes in them and the sharing of one's gifts;
- an acceptance of self, with its riches and limitations;
- self-discipline that fosters independence and respect for others;
- patience that leads to respect for personal growth;
- willingness to take on one's social responsibilities.

Goal V
Personal Growth in an Atmosphere of Wise Freedom
Criteria
1. Genuine concern for each member of the school community is a priority.
2. Students learn to deal with their gifts and limitations in a growth-producing way.
3. Students are helped to share their knowledge and gifts with others.
4. School policies and practices further the development of self-discipline.
5. The school provides for the development of leadership.

The last Goal is rooted in the principles of mutuality and sharing. It is especially important in its concern for those young people called upon to exercise "leadership." Likewise, "the sharing of knowledge and gifts with others" is a concrete expression of esteem for others, and it contributes to building a community whose goal is to bring these concerns to fruition. "To commit oneself actively" and "effectively" to a world reeling from oppression and injustice leads to a process by which life's meaning can be affirmed and a sense of hope can be fostered.

Taken together, the Goals and Criteria are a common framework for a variety of projects. The interplay of the personal and the universal, of the familiar and the other, is the warp and weft; uniformity no longer enjoys the place of honor. The transmission of educational identity involves careful consideration of tradition, its values and its objectives. All of this is then brought to life within the national and international network of Sacred Heart Schools. The character of this education is given new expression; as at the "beginning," it takes fully into account the original charism.

Nevertheless, this charism reveals other themes as well. Encounter, solidarity and mutual responsibility, sharing and creativity, liberation and justice are its highlighted ideas. Collaboration and evaluation govern its application. The same holds true for the integration of contemporary social sciences and the humanities. The expression "*cor unum*," so dear to tradition, is now expressed in the language of interdependence, in a way that "permits each school as well as the network to function in an optimal fashion." This worldwide openness has found its framework in the global nature of the institute and its understanding of education, the criteria by which any educational practice should be judged.

Another characteristic, and certainly not a negligible one, is openness to transcendence.[193] A new "image" is substituted for the former shield emblazoned on the boarding schools: the figure of Christ, servant. The educational approach aims

---

193 This is made explicit in the first four criteria of Goal I; in the sixth criterion of Goal II; and in the second criterion of Goal IV.

to recognize this transcendence within the world of human existence (Goal I). The discovery is that of an encounter. It implies a thorough intellectual development that includes recent scientific and technical discoveries. It presupposes an intellectual openness and an appetite for learning (Goal II). Its purpose is to reinforce life's meaning to foster hope. This goal is met through relationships and community involvement, thanks to the mastery of the right skills (Goals III, IV and V). The chief beneficiary is the student: his or her training will open up a future to be lived with and for others.

At this first time when the institute began its renewal, the source of its energy to modernize and adapt its educational work could be clearly seen. Joined to new circumstances and new participants, the charism of union and conformity with the Heart of Christ opens up a new way forward. The Chapter of 1964 set in motion the canonical conditions that made it possible: the ending of conventual cloister. This important factor by itself was not enough. Canon law may have delineated, opened or limited new, modernized practices, but the real force was a spirituality that responded to appeals beyond the old frontiers.

CHAPTER II

When the Metaphor of the River Comes to Life

THE CHOICE OF EDUCATION as the Institute's service had been reaffirmed. Nevertheless, resistance and misunderstanding gathered around how to interpret the original goal, expressed now in terms of justice, sharing, and liberation. Confusion remained in the minds of some religious: what meaning would be accorded to *the primordial idea of the Society*? Around what central idea would the work of education be developed? Would any consensus be possible, given the diversity of cultural perspectives, ways of life, and ideologies?

To review the process by which the educational goals were understood is to be invited to witness, to see how a metaphor comes to life when the image returns to its biblical roots. In other words, it follows a path leading back to the source: the Word that, alone, ontologically, is the original act capable of regeneration, of making life truly "new." The stakes are real. Cultural shifts happen at the level of images, along the spectrum of a spiritual sensibility where individual and collective strength stores its vital energy and its power of social cohesion.

The path followed by the development of this biblical symbol parallels the starts and stops of the approach taken by the community. *Toward the River Whose Source is in the East* (Section 1) presents the biblically rooted movement of the original symbol. *The Collective Interpretation of the Initial Educational Goals* (Section 2) describes the long process at the end of which the orientations of 1970 were ratified and the educational purpose recodified.

II.1 Toward the River Whose Source Is in the East

The collection[194] of 47 circular letters written by Concepción Camacho comprises a narrative of institutional renewal. To judge from their dates, 1970 to 1982, one might be tempted to think that the whole of the document is directed toward achieving *aggiornamento* and writing the new Constitutions, a not entirely false conclusion. Such an interpretation can be made because Circular Letters 1 through 37 constitute a set meant to prepare for the writing of the 1982 Constitutions. It should be noted that two of these letters (1 and 37) are the only ones addressed to each and every religious. This fact highlights each woman's personal involvement and responsibility, traditionally expressed in the words: "The fate of the Society is in our hands." These two signs might lead us to this conclusion. But another reading makes us conclude that this entity arises from a metaphor, which is at first hinted at cautiously, then seems to

---

194 *Letters to the Society,* Concepción Camacho, RSCJ, Superior General of the Society of the Sacred Heart of Jesus, 1970–1982. Tipografia Poliglotta della Pontifica Università Gregoriana, Rome, 1992.

vanish,[195] and ultimately appears clearly in the forty-sixth letter.

When Poverty Is Synonymous with Hope
In order to interpret the original goals, one must step back from the "already known." To do this requires a particular mindset: one must have a poor heart; that is to say, one must abandon paternalistic and ethnocentric attitudes and appreciate different cultures. Concepción Camacho, elected superior general at the end of Chapter 1970, drew people in through the power of suggestion. She reread the group's experience, taking as her point of departure this passage from the Gospel of St. John: "When Jesus looked up and saw a great crowd coming toward him, he said to Philip: 'Where shall we buy bread for these people to eat?' He asked only to test him, for he already had in mind what he was going to do." John 6: 5-6. Like the disciples, we are poised to make concrete decisions. We do not lack confidence. But if we are to live in union and conformity with the "dispositions" of Christ, we must assume a poverty of heart. Such poverty opens one toward internationality, toward a sense of mutual aid and reciprocity, toward concern for "those who suffer."[196]

Using new language, a paragraph from the summary of the 1815 Constitutions on the spirit of poverty was thus interpreted.[197] Vulnerability and the stripping away of one's own culture were the expressions chosen, for "poverty is of the same substance as hope." From the perspective of the Institute's "primordial idea," the place where the living God might truly be

---

195 According to J.-Y. Pouilloux, such a route is typical of metaphor, Encyclopedia Universalis, *Article: Métaphore*, Corpus 15, Paris 1996, p. 184-5.

196 *Letters to the Society,* Concepción Camacho, p. 61.

197 Constitutions, *Society of the Sacred Heart of Jesus*, Summary, 339. X., p. 143-4.

adored emerges out of the social realities of the contemporary world: "It is up to the community to open itself routinely to secularization as a paradox that might lead it to live more fully in the presence of God, and to see God everywhere." This point of view calls for discernment.

These qualifications are set forth: to live internationality with a concern for understanding others and mutually supporting one another; to allow oneself to be shaped by the spirit of Christ in order to be open to the cry of our brothers and sisters; to be those who share their bread and fish with one another and in so doing become "adorers in spirit and in truth." The process would be long, for such transformation concerned both habits of behavior and a collective imagination in which notions of one nation's superiority over another had deep roots. A new form of religious life was on the horizon. Its harbinger would be interior poverty, an expression of hope like that of the open heart—available and vulnerable, like that of the poor.

Return to the Source

The first three letters reveal the challenge that immediately confronted the process of renewal.

As with the cornerstone of Saint Ignatius Loyola's Spiritual Exercises, the narrative describes, from the opening letter, a three-pronged relationship among the world, Christ, and the educational community of the Religious of the Sacred Heart. It offers an international overview: whatever the reason for a given letter, its scope includes events, persons met, and recognized needs. After visiting India and Egypt, the members of the Central Team traveled to France, North America and Latin America. In 1972, they toured the provinces of Australia/New

Zealand, Spain, Holland and Ireland/Scotland, Peru and Chili, Argentina-Uruguay, and Brazil.

The use of the river metaphor appeared in four letters that can be grouped in three sets (5, 26 and 37 taken together, and 46) that reveal three stages in the interpretive process (1970 to 1976; 1976 to 1979; 1979 to 1982).

Letter 5 offers a way for people to think about reality. In conveying it, the writing uses—for the first time—the biblical metaphor of the spring. In France, in Joigny, the superior general and her team "felt the Society's life force in the freshness of its primitive spirit." They "prayed and reflected on the silent strength of the water that sprang directly from the source: the very center of the person of Jesus, his Heart." Beneath the surface, one could see that this expression is rooted in the gospel of St. John. Then, at once, like a waterfall, understanding and emotion were aroused: "and we recognized, marveling, the secret power of a poor, humble, hidden source." The image of the spring returns here with the adjectives "humble and hidden" and grounds the metaphor in its origin.

When the history and societal beginnings of this metaphor are set forth, the message's essential meaning emerges: Jesus, God made flesh, who assumes and transforms all human life and who loves us above all other aspects of creation, invites us to "remain in his love." We can see that the charism of the congregation has been stated strongly and simply. The mention of Jesus recalls the fragility of a precarious birth in a Bethlehem stable and the uniqueness of his family. Putting it this way points to the universality of salvation: "God made man who takes on and transforms all human life." It makes visible the figure of Christ, source of life—He who initiates union and invites us to an assured closeness, suggesting the freedom that love brings with it. The circumstances refer to the beginning of all things: the word of the Son, alone capable of true conversion, of a transformation that is authentic re-birth, in faithfulness to the source.

To make of the past a living present brought us renewed responsibility. And questions arose from every corner: "How do we make this love visible in today's world? How do we remain faithful to the evangelical call of our origins?" Apprehension resurfaced, and a series of questions emerged whose focus circled around the consistency of an educational ethic:

We must ask ourselves about these personal and communitarian choices:

Do they correspond to the purposes that we have put forward?

Are we concerned for those human beings who are the most neglected, the most forgotten?

Do we have sufficient courage to sustain a patient effort to accompany the others in their search?

Do we know how to recognize and appreciate what other cultures have to tell us about Christ?

Are we capable of discovering and assuming the forms of poverty that surround us?

Through its power to suggest, the symbol of the spring supported the questioning and the search.

This experience, related with simplicity and energy, expressed an identity: to know – to indwell – to make love visible. Missionary methods were proposed; the chosen recipients were identified. Thus, a way to bring this about was outlined.

One year later, Letter 6 spelled out the central challenge facing educators: injustice. In 1967, the scourge to be combated was hunger and ignorance. In 1970, in a "divided, broken world,"[198] the Society of the Sacred Heart committed itself to "respond to the needs of all human beings oppressed by ignorance and servitude, and above all to those young people who seek a meaning in life." Letter 11 describes an advance on several fronts: collaboration with the local Church and other congregations, an expansion in the orientations of educational institutes, consideration of today's realities in connection with Christ's attitudes toward the poor and marginalized.[199] A gradual engagement with the social realities of the day and a new relationship with the environment was coming to fruition.

This new mode of apostolic life, far from the restrictive protections of the convent, led to the appearance of a new theme on the missionary horizon: solidarity in situations of injustice. Letter 12 offers a theological basis for this orientation. In following Christ, we must "preach the Good News to the poor, heal the brokenhearted, announce that captives shall be released and the blind shall see, that the downtrodden shall be released from their oppressors."[200] Because "the reality of mission must be the creating, liberating power of Jesus who alone can give us the strength to be open to the Spirit who enables us to struggle against injustice and who 'makes all things new.'"[201] Seven years

---

198 *Society of the Sacred Heart, Chapter of 1970,* Rome, p. 10, 12.

199 *Letters to the Society,* Concepción Camacho, Letter 11, 20 October 1972, p. 25.

200 Gospel of Luke, 4, 18, quoting Isaiah 61, 1.

201 *Letters to the Society,* Concepción Camacho, Letter 12, 15 December 1972, pp. 27-8.

later, this evangelical priority would become established as the goal of the educational program.

Water that Flows from the Source

A second round of institutional renewal appears in Letters 26 and 37. Indeed, the metaphor of the river occurs for the first time in May 1977, in Letter 26. A full transcription of this passage will show the force of its message as well as the charm of its style:

> I would like to end this letter by summarizing my experience in a single image:
> I asked myself first how and where the river ought to flow.
> Later I understood that the important thing is for the river to have water.
> In Joigny I found its source.
> Throughout my journey, I was able to feel that the water is already alive and flowing.
> And so my letter comes full of joy.[202]

The text, in and of itself, needs no commentary. Above all, the date is significant: this letter was written six months after the Chapter of 1976, whose objective was to discern an institutional identity, to understand "how to glorify the Heart of Jesus Christ, suffering in the midst of humanity."[203] A significant step forward had been made. The joy and serenity of the letter offer the proof of it. A border had been crossed: the process of renewal could

---

202 *Letters to the Society,* Concepción Camacho, Letter 26, 25 May 1977, p. 64
203 *Letters to the Society,* Concepción Camacho Letter 37, 25 March 1980, p. 92.

now proceed. The superior general exhorts her audience in these terms: "I have seen that the strength of his love is for all ages. 'The thoughts of his heart are to all generations.' Ps.33. May his flame purify us, free us from the rigidity which may have resulted from the passage of time."

Four years later, on March 25, 1980, a final phase of the collective work was announced. Two instructions were issued: to meditate on the work of future Constitutions, and to identify anything that might prevent them from being freely accepted. As Joseph Varin had understood at sensitive moments during the early years, it was essential when foundational renewal was taking place to distance oneself from the problems of the moment and to identify any opposition or resistance in order to proceed with true discernment.

Letter 37 presents, above all, a new rootedness in the Bible. Addressed, as is Letter 1, to every member of the Society, it accompanied the preparatory documents for the new Constitutions. The superior general opens by highlighting the collective implications. Then she compares the Society to "the tree planted by the bank [that] stretches its roots along the stream. . . . In a year of drought it has no fear, and does not cease to bear fruit" (Jer 17:8). In effect, if the evangelical call of the Religious of the Sacred Heart expresses itself today in a world marked by constant change, there is no need to be fearful. Because the educational goal "is rooted in the living stream of Scripture and in Saint Madeleine Sophie's intuitive desire to make known, in Jesus Christ, the love and glory of God, 'compassionate and gracious, . . . ever constant and true' (Ex.34.6)."

The evocation of the spring, in letters 5 and 26, had successfully employed two referents: the intuition of Sophie Barat and the biblical word. Here, the metaphor connects them. Had the founding symbol finally discovered its native soil and—through that—its vitality?

The River That Runs through History

This biblical rootedness did not emerge until 1982,[204] just before the General Chapter, at which new Constitutions were to be written. In a simple and straightforward style, Letter 46 transmits a familiar way of looking at reality. Its interpretation of what has happened is more precise, a model—as if Concepción Camacho, one last time before her generalate ended, wanted to suggest a way to look contemplatively at reality. The framework is the same as that conveyed in Letter 5, but the accent is now placed on *seeing* it. The words spill out and overflow:

> I looked... It brought vividly to mind the image of the spring of water, which gives life to the Society.
> I saw...
> Then I remembered two situations I have lived during my last trips, two situations that are critical for today's world: Nicaragua and Poland.
> In these two countries, I experienced in a special way the strength that comes from that Spring of Water. I observed how living faith can lead to the gift of self, and to the collaboration with a humble, generous and patient Church.

---

204 *Letters to the Society*, Concepción Camacho, Letter 46, 4 May 1982, p. 113.

The words of Psalm 32 took on new meaning: "The Lord brings the counsel of the nations to naught; he frustrates the plans of the peoples. The counsel of the Lord stands forever, the thoughts of his heart to all generations."

Then the stirring metaphor emerges: "These thoughts of love and liberation are the work of his compassionate Heart, that stream of water which runs through history, that action which is salvation for all who hope." This biblical symbol provides the ultimate dimension that makes it possible to avoid any anthropomorphism. The metaphorical language[205] links with one precise stroke the sign and the signifier, the concept and the image. And the statement is now expanded. It is now accompanied by the summation of a treasure to share with a kind of urgency that is present in the metaphor:

> I realized anew that the contemplation of the Body of Christ, of humanity, of the world around us, takes us out of ourselves and leads us to the gift of self; it is a saving way. I understood that by our vocation these words are spoken in a special way to us: "See my hands and my feet, that it is I myself." (Lk.34,39) Only by being vulnerable, by letting ourselves be touched by the sufferings of his Body, can we give a real response to the needs of the world. I can never insist enough on the need for contemplation that our apostolic life carries with it. "We cannot glorify the adorable Heart of Jesus worthily save inasmuch as we apply ourselves to study its interior dispositions in order to unite and conform ourselves to

---

205 Encyclopedia Universalis. According to J.-Y. Pouilloux, this language is a "privileged expression for our times," p. 184.

them." (Const. 5) Only thus will our love transform our lives and the lives of others.

The "hidden treasure" of his Heart is thereby revealed: the force that gave birth to the apostolic Institute is the river of living water that flows through history, announced by the prophet Zachariah. The open Heart of Christ is identified with this river, beside which the verdant tree gives fruit in every season.[206] "Come, everyone who is thirsty, to the waters; come those who desire it, drink freely from the springs of living water." The "return to the source," the original intuition of Sophie Barat, is here carried out. The collection of letters might now be brought to a close.

II.2 The Collective Interpretation of the Original Educational Goals

The route of the biblical symbol's elaboration paralleled the deadlocks and advances in the collective interpretation of the original educational goals. In fact, translating the concept of *reparation* into terms of liberation and justice did not sit well with those whose spirituality remained strongly tied to the imprint of Paray-le-Monial. Nevertheless, in 1976 the key element of the Society's symbolism—the Heart of Christ—underwent a shift. And between 1980 and 1982, a "healing of the collective memory" occurred, which consisted of rediscovering "the

---

206 Revelation 22,2.

deeper sense of authentic adoration."²⁰⁷

Additional resistance arose from people's difficulty accepting a "redistribution"²⁰⁸ of the decision-making power. The provinces of Western Europe had in the past been at the center of such directives as the plans of studies. However, beginning in 1967, the impetus came from the American continent. Contrary to what Mme. de Gramont d'Aster²⁰⁹ had once asserted, the Society of the Sacred Heart was not intrinsically French or European; in 1982, a renewed sense of internationality was clear in the calm acceptance of these new orientations.

Consensus arrived at the moment when the metaphor had finally made itself truly felt. This fact confirmed Jean-Yves Fouilloux' assertion: "We can access a new reality only when—through that reality and only through it—we are able to resist forgetting."²¹⁰ To liberate memory means returning to the source of a "living" word.

---

207 Between 1980 and 1982, the number of circular letters accelerated. Their quantity reveals a delicate moment, one that required both the participation of the greatest number of people, and a means to communicate how life was currently being lived across the provinces. This was no small challenge, given that the field whereon the metaphor was being expressed and developed was the field of action.

208 Under the direction of J.-M. Mayeur, L. Pietri, A. Vauchez, M. Venard, *Histoire du Christianisme,* Tome 13, Crises et Renouveau (de 1958 à nos jours), Chapitre VII, Crises et mutations de la mission chrétienne par C. Prudhomme et J.F. Zorn, Desciée, 2000, p. 355.

209 Tr. Note: Eugénie de Gramont, RSCJ, the daughter of one of Marie Antoinette's ladies-in-waiting and a member of one of France's oldest aristocratic families, ran the Paris school for many years. During the years 1839-41, she was a vocal member of the French faction in a power struggle involving Rome and the French bishops, which came close to splitting the Society.

210 *Letters to the Society,* Concepción Camacho, p. 186.

A Shifting of the Symbolic

The 1970 General Chapter had already expressed it in these terms: "To contemplate his Heart we have no need to turn away from this earth, the home of God made Man. Christ is present, hidden in the heart of the world. Earth could not hold him in death; he lives and the whole world of time and space is transfigured through his risen life."[211] These words reflect a shift in the central challenge. In a cloistered world, and in accordance with the symbolism of the center that related to it,[212] the ritual of adoring a living God was essentially carried out in the place of worship. From now on, however, it could be carried out elsewhere, updating the original idea: "It is among humanity, with whom he shared his fear, his loneliness, and his love, that his glory shines forth." The place of contemplation has become the place of action.

This interpretation was reconfirmed at the 1976 General Chapter in an unprecedented way. The two challenges were seen in relationship: yesterday, godlessness; today, injustice.

Saint Madeleine Sophie, listening to the calls of her day, saw the Body of Christ "outraged" by "impiety"; today we contemplate the wounded Heart of Christ in his Body, torn apart by the injustices of the world; our charism urges us to be one with men in their sufferings and in their quest for a more just and fraternal world."[213]

---

211 Society of the Sacred Heart, *1970 Chapter*, Rome, p. 56.
212 See Mircea Eliade, *Images et symboles*, Ch. I, Paris, Gallimard, NRF, 1952, p. 33-72.
213 Society of the Sacred Heart, *1976 Chapter*, Charism, p. 19-20.

Whether then or now, the challenge is the same. The humanity of Christ has been stricken in that aspect which constitutes his unlimited dignity. The key to interpreting it, theologically speaking, is the Covenant between Christ and humanity. Therein "is the hidden mystery, which evolves within history." The General Chapter, adhering faithfully to the original plan, in this way records the shift.

A Well-Ordered Decision-Making Process

The new relationship with a world torn by injustice awakened compassion through contact with a wounded humanity: "His heart, opened, shows us the way. He calls on us each day to be in communion with the sufferings of humanity; he continues to urge us to struggle against egoism, sharing with our brothers in the sorrow caused by injustice and evil."[214] This spiritual intention replaced the "horror" felt before the "outrages" and "ingratitude" of men referenced in the Constitutions of 1815. In conjunction with the awareness of violated human dignity, it governed the commitment: "In a world that does not reflect the standards of the Kingdom, and where humans are often used, disfigured, and deprived of their most basic needs," it was a question of "seeking solidarity with the poor and marginalized, and collaborating in our mutual liberation made of a growth in faith and love." In the face of the "unjust and dehumanizing structures of our world (. . .), the need 'to embrace all the means within our power" was the order of the day. The invitation to assume the mantle of Christ with respect to the poor and marginalized clarified the discernment.

---

214 *Letters to the Society*, Concepción Camacho, Letter 8, March 1972, p. 16.

An active solidarity was reaffirmed. During this phase of the Institute's renewal, for those whose eyes saw God in a humanity wounded by injustice, it flowed faithfully from the original insights. To commune with the suffering of humanity and to combat forms of evil became the modern expression of a charism in union and conformity with the Heart of Christ. This kind of consensus became the most important guideline for initiatives.

In 1815, the Christian education of young women sought a commitment to the "harm" undergone, an awakening of conscience that prompted a sense of generosity. Such "horrifying ingratitude" called for a form of intervention that was shaped by the strength of the feelings experienced. The "reparation" was at once spiritual and social. It was an "obligatory" vehicle, necessary for restoring the honor of a subject that had been outraged, humiliated, devalued. The spiritual process involved three aspects whose relationship might be diagrammed as follows:

see the outrage	→	feel it
act on it		
repair it, compensate for it		

These three elements (the outrage committed against Christ by humanity; a sense of the dignity and suffering of humanity; action or reparation) can be traced back to the narrative of the *Original Idea* of the Institute. They even contributed to its formation.

Let us take up the text briefly once again, in order to discover this decision-making process. "In emerging from the Terror," Sophie Barat meditated on the "abominations of the Revolution with respect to religion and the Blessed Sacrament." She felt an urgency to "make Jesus Christ come back to life" within families. She considered the different ways that could be followed by "hearts that remained faithful to God": to reestablish the worship of the Blessed Sacrament, to provide for the clergy, to support the bishops. Her entire self was engaged in this experience, her sensibilities deeply affected. Her imagination, fully engaged, became creative. A movement was agreed on. A new pathway to serving and loving a living God opened as a result of this discernment.[215] The image of "millions of adorers before a universal monstrance" summarized the response that accompanied this movement. Sophie Barat abandoned her plan for a monastic life because she was deeply affected by the godlessness of society in post-Revolutionary France.

Philippine Duchesne was well aware of such shifts and displacements. She was not to go to China, but Louisiana; not to Saint Louis, but Saint Charles. In evoking the behavior of Philippine and her first companions on the American continent, María Josefa Bultó highlighted two aptitudes: a capacity to "see" the educational needs of the time and place, and adaptability. "Faced with a superhuman task," she said, "she was constantly learning, improvising, seeking solutions to recurring needs or to new problems.... She saw the needs of her day, and tried to fulfill them within her own call to the Society."[216]

The analogy between the missionary awakening of Sacred Heart students and the creative inspiration of Sophie Barat is significant in the sense that it is marked by a particular approach

---

215 P. Perdrau, *Les loisirs de l'Abbaye*, Rome, A.S-C.F., p. 422-423.
216 *Letters to the Society,* Concepción Camacho, Letter 5, p. 73-74.

to life, a way of confronting reality and inserting oneself into it. The key factor determining one's action is awareness of the emotion felt in contemplating that reality. The mediating element is the spiritual emotion: compassion.

This decision-making path also marked the collective process of renewal. One sees this over and over again in the documents. The new goal, "to work for justice," resulted from the interaction between the contact with social reality and the goals of the Institute. The wound that affects Christ's humanity today is that of men and women broken by injustice. This process might be represented according to the same rationale expressed in Sophie Barat's original idea:

See	Ally oneself
Human beings exploited, disfigured frustrated in their needs and aspirations	with human beings in their sufferings
Act =	
Work for justice	
Work for human growth and liberation	
Work for a more just, fraternal world	

From now on, "to carry out what Saint Madeleine Sophie understood by the expression the glory of the Heart of Jesus" involved this struggle for justice. Solidarity, under the paired aspects of compassion and social engagement, was ordered around this end. And it was confirmed as follows: "We can continue the incarnation of Jesus Christ in the world, we can let the Father glorify his Son in us. . . We can incarnate those attitudes which will enable God to show himself."²¹⁷

To work for justice thereby receives the same approval as reparation. In the same way, to encounter the world's wounded and marginalized followed the tradition faithfully. In sketching the portrait of the first religious of the Institute, Mgr. Baunard highlighted, in effect, two separate traits:

> Some, previously devoted to exterior works and moved by the needs of the world they encountered, sought in religious life the opportunity to do apostolic work. What these religious saw in the Heart of Christ was above all the flames that emanate from it to give warmth and comfort to the world. The others, previously inclined toward the contemplative life of Carmel or the Poor Clares or even the Trappists, were more moved by the outrages done to the Heart of Christ. It was his wound that they contemplated, and they wished to hide within it a life of reparation, contemplation, and love.²¹⁸

The sketch ends with a remark that makes sense: "To burn and illuminate, to consume oneself in love, to spread oneself in zeal: such is the double purpose that, within the Society whose history we are writing, will continue to take shape more and more every day."²¹⁹ In this period of renewal, to empathize and

---

217 *Letters to the Society,* Concepción Camacho, Letter 23, November 14, 1976, p. 56.

218 These two aspects were symbolized in the institutional seal: the sword that pierces the heart of the Virgin Mary and the flame of love situated above the heart of Christ.

219 Mgr Baunard, *Histoire de la Vénérable M.-S. Barat fondatrice de la Société du Sacré Cœur de Jésus,* Livre I, Chap. III, Poussielgue Frères, 4è éd., Paris, 1879, p. 97-98.

be one with, to heal wounds and open a pathway where life is shown to have meaning—these are the two constituent goals of a single educational purpose. The new missionary challenge, that of engagement, has for its purpose to gather together what has become disconnected. Such is the pathway that, today, the successful application of the image has taken.

"Education for Justice in Faith"
Following the trajectory begun in 1967, the validation of the educational goals came to completion in January of 1979. The document drafted by the provincials, meeting in Mexico, opened by reminding everyone of the assembly's objective: "to clarify, according to what is lived out in the provinces, the work of education." It was decided, after evaluating the educational practice, that

> "We affirm as our educational work, today,
> EDUCATION FOR JUSTICE IN FAITH."

In order to pursue this direction, it is necessary:
- to regard the world with Jesus' preferential love for the poor and marginalized, a preference that should mark our lives there where we are.
- to see humanity as the children of God and brothers and sisters in Jesus Christ, called to live and to develop our humanity according to the Gospel.
- to live a Faith that is inseparable from engagement with reality.

These conditions of fulfillment evoke a way of being and acting whose model is the figure of Christ in relationship with his Father and with the destitute of this world.

The original institutional choice was reaffirmed: to concentrate on persons likely to become agents of social transformation. The novelty lay in the fact that this orientation also involved the poor and marginalized. The following groups were selected:
- Youth
- Women
- Families
- Influencers
- Baseline Communities

This group was inspired by the diversity of cultures encountered and the historical moment being lived in those countries where Religious of the Sacred Heart were working. Internationality was identified as a treasured resource and a stimulus to creativity.

Criteria were organized under six rubrics: "response to needs, education, visible community of faith, regard for the Church, regard for the apostolic body, financial realism." They were seen as points of departure for institutional choices. In fact, it all had to do with attitudes, educational objectives, or institutional goals. Following is the list of criteria for the rubric of "education":
- to aim to form the whole person;
- to develop attitudes of love and respect toward people considered to be different;
- to create a community in which people educate one another;
- to help the person to be the agent of his or her own growth within a dynamic process;

- to develop freedom and solidarity, service toward others, responsibility and a sense of commitment, liberty and a critical understanding that values choices made in accordance with the Gospel, creativity in the face of reality;
- to permit the person to be an agent of transformation;
- to seek to build Communion lived in a spirit of forgiveness and reconciliation.

These criteria served both to develop educational projects and to evaluate educational practice. Transferable from one project to the next, from one learning situation to another, they fostered creativity.

Whatever the rubric, solidarity was developed within the paradigm of communion, practiced in terms of relationship, openness, justice, collaboration, and sharing. It brought life to the "mission of making manifest the love of God made human." When applied to the rubric of education, it had the value of an educational objective; applied to a community of faith, it expressed itself as an evangelical call. Some directives that appeared in 1967, the diversity of cultures and collaboration, referred to it as well. They serve as an element that characterizes the educational environment or methodology.

Concise and open, the text closed with an invitation to each province to find ways to put it into practice. Three resources were suggested: ongoing formation, evaluation, biblical and theological study.

Twelve years after the 1967 Special Chapter, this educational directive was a response to the "cry" then heard. The new missionary challenge—to go out and encounter a humanity wounded by injustice—became functional within an educational plan in use throughout the world.

To Recognize the Presence of the Living God

In 1982, another stage of the process of renovation was carried out. Just before the writing of the new Constitutions, a consensus was reached on the interpretation of the original spiritual goal: to shape adorers. Circular Letter 41 puts it in these terms: a new esteem for education, understood as "a service that helps people feel they are children of God and collaborators in the building of a more just world," came to light. "To convey the grandeur, the tenderness, and the benevolence of God" became once again the goal around which the work of education was structured.

To make explicit what had been rediscovered, the superior general related an international encounter she had experienced on May 25, 1981: "We shared what we thought Saint Madeleine Sophie would say to our world today." In the various exchanges that took place, one observation was unanimous: "The world situation impels us to offer what we can: the powerful love of Jesus Christ, which leads to adoration of the living God." And she makes the following quite clear: "Adoration is inseparable from the effort to bring light into a world where people live in greater communion." To collaborate in the humanization of society implies adoration as a principle of effectiveness. In order to accomplish this, a specific way of being is required: "Freedom and clarity of those who participate in the power of the risen Jesus, free from all sectarianism." This evangelical simplicity comes to us from Christ, the sole "adorer of the Father, in spirit and in truth."

The target population is youth. "The most urgent need is to respond to people's deepest aspirations: help them seek and find the meaning in their lives, the reasons for their hope and the strength of love."[220] Such is the lived experience. It interprets, in today's language, one of the educational goals of the founding plan.

This "living page" is unprecedented in its establishment of a link between adoration and the discovery of a meaning to existence. An intrinsic link, if one judges by its chief assertion: adoration cannot be separated from social engagement, from an action with missionary purpose. The Constitutions of 1982 express it as follows: "To cast light on the Love of God revealed, whose Heart of Christ is for us the source and the symbol."

To be touched by the mystery of the open side of Christ nurtures an awareness of the absolute dignity of humanity. Because such an encounter is the unveiling of the grandeur of being human, called to participate in everlasting life and to become an instigator of social change. As Letter 41 indicates, the foundation of community involvement is the discovery of "this hidden treasure that makes itself known, little by little, within history." The following diagram illustrates the process described in the letter:

A new awareness of the dignity of every human being
A higher estimation of the other = to believe in his or her possibilities
To create spaces wherein he or she might discover these possibilities
and unlock them for others

---

220 *Letters to the Society,* Concepción Camacho, Letter 41, June 5, 1981, p. 102-104.

Is this not what Father Druilhet meant when he described the vocation of students and Religious of the Sacred Heart as "noble and sublime"? The task was noble because of its goal. Because restoration concerns the very image that humans have of themselves. However, such an image is deeply embedded, there where the heart—in the biblical sense of that term—lies. If this place is fathomless, in the sense that it is made up of the very thing that grounds it, then it becomes the connection between the human and the divine. It is, in the words of St. Thomas Aquinas, "at the very border of the spiritual and material worlds."

"To shape adorers and repairers" is thus one and the same thing. The goal is single, unique, though the spiritual dynamic might be analyzed on two levels—one cognitive and one social. The first level involves the awakening of an awareness of divinity in the other person, a recognition of transcendence within cultural mediations. The second is that of action, where it is a question of forming a conscience enlightened by faith, one capable of discerning, of engaging itself with a view toward transforming society.

"Adoration is the movement by which we recognize the presence of God within our world, where we allow his love to exert power over our life." In this sense, to love one's brothers and sisters is not to dissociate oneself from the acknowledgement of the lordship of Christ. It is a component of the act of adoration, the prolongation of its expression. Within the spirituality of the Sacred Heart, it takes on the face of compassion and service. To make known the ultimate destiny of the human being, to develop an enlightened Faith in a world marked by the atheism of the Enlightenment, was the educational goal of the schools of the Sacred Heart in the 19th century.[221] Even today, such is the freely given gift to be recognized and shared, the promise that flows from the "open Side of Jesus."[222]

New Wineskins for New Wine

In 1982, the fundamental renovation of the work of education was accompanied by a new design for the Society's identifying image: the logo replaced the traditional seal.

From 1815 to 1980, the original symbol had been the image of the two Hearts of Jesus and Mary:

The Heart of Jesus, in which one sees the wound, surrounded by a crown of thorns, the cross implanted in this heart, the flames expressing love.

The Heart of Mary, slightly in the background, and so one with that of Jesus, also pierced by the sword (prophesied by Simeon) and emanating flames of love.

Above it, the Eucharistic host, beaming with light and expressing the close bond that Madeleine Sophie Barat always felt between the Eucharist and the Sacred Heart.

Around it, the fleur de lys, symbol of the purity of the heart that unites itself with Redemption."[223]

---

221 It was at that time formulated in analogous terms: "to make known to the world the treasures of his heart and to prepare Him a generation full of faith, by planting the germ of this faith in the young students confided to your care, which will one day increase a hundredfold."

222 Constitutions of 1982, p. 168

223 Ouvrage collectif, *Religieuses du Sacré Cœur*, A. Bigo, Ed. du Signe, Strasbourg, 1999, p. 14.

This representation was classic in the 19th century: "This image conveys that the object of Eucharistic adoration is Jesus giving his life for love of us."

Along with the new status accorded to religious apostolic life and a new relationship with the world appeared a new symbol. At the center of the image is a drawing of a world map surrounded by a stylized heart. A small cross, situated at the opening of the heart, represents a passageway to a world beyond the terrestrial. Centered on the idea of interiority, the logo opens itself to infinite hope. If realistic, the figure of the heart would be closed, but it is here symbolically left open. The broad opening invites entry to the Unrestricted.

Vulnerability, suggested by the drawing of the cross and the openness of the heart, is necessary to the adoration of the living God, just as it is in the fight for justice. It is what allows for the release, within the intimacy of a human being, of a wellspring: the charism of union and conformity with the Heart of Christ. It also evokes a kind of poverty, which consists of welcoming of and esteem for other cultures, exchange and ability to collaborate, compassion lived in a committed interdependence. These traits speak to an allegiance "in name and in deed to a gentle and humble Christ."

From 1976 to 1982, the collective interpretation had avoided dogmatism, and consensus on educational goals was reached at the General Chapters. What followed corroborated this consensus. But from a critical point of view, it remained to be seen whether the second organizing principle of the original educational plan—the rule of dividing pupils into classes or grades for studies in the humanities—had been the object of shared thought. This requirement for admission guaranteed the phased learning of the French language and allowed students, over the long term, to reach a major educational goal: to express oneself with ease and elegance in order to transmit Christian values. The study of rhetoric, natural history, and cosmology constituted the prerequisite for thinking for oneself and finding one's independent and mature place in family and social life.

These foundations characterized the education of Sacred Heart students until 1967. After the 1852 Plan of Studies, written by Aimée d'Avenas,[224] and the books written by Janet Erskine Stuart,[225] a collective work—*The Spirit and Plan of Studies*[226]—had characterized the education until 1967. It

---

224 The introduction to the 1852 Plan of Studies, written by Aimée d'Avenas, singles out two parameters: the development of intelligence and discernment.

225 Janet Erskine Stuart, *The Education of Catholic Girls* and *The Society of the Sacred Heart*, London, 1923, A.S-C.F.

226 Ouvrage collectif, *Esprit et plan des études dans la Société du Sacré-Cœur de Jésus*, Typis polyglottis vaticanis, 1954.

offered a reinterpretation of the organization of the humanities on three levels: logic in the second class [third academic], psychology in the first class [fourth academic], and philosophy in superior class.

Would this integrating principle of the course of studies remain in place? If yes, how would it be translated, and how would it be aligned with the spiritual and social goals?

CHAPTER III

Constitutive Principles of Education in the Society of the Sacred Heart

SPACE AND TIME ARE THE CONSTITUENT DIMENSIONS of every human life. They can be found in the preamble to the original plan of studies: "The success of a plan of studies depends essentially on the allocation of time wisely managed, the order of exercises, and the style of teaching." The organization of every academic year is spread over a literary and cultural space; the way learning is organized must follow the rule of "gradus," applied throughout one's academic career.

In the new version, the defined space is that of relationship; from now on the "fourth means" of the 1815 Constitutions, "relationships with persons from the outside," characterizes every educational activity. It has become the meeting place for many different learning activities. And if the key skill remains an ability to communicate, it is no longer accomplished via the rules of rhetoric. The art of discourse has been supplanted by that of the "encounter."

The ultimate goal remains the capacity to discern according to evangelical values in a way that creates just relations with people, things, and nature. This assures the consistency of training projects; its purpose is to help achieve the spiritual goal. It is why the pace of scholarly life here is called *practical wisdom* or *ethical goal*. And the very idea of time is translated in terms of a *pathway*. In fact, if time implies a process of growth, a pathway indicates rather an itinerary to travel along with others. Its uniqueness becomes open to different ways of organizing training.

"Respect, a Space Where Encounter Can Occur" (first section) points to the original educational ethic of the Society of the Sacred Heart. "A Pathway: to Discern in order to Accomplish Justice with Humility" (second section) outlines the rule's having become essential, following the spirit of the original plan. "In Memory of the Alliance" (section three) establishes the frame of reference to be used in order to assure the unity of the educational plans in all of their diversity.

III.1 Respect, the Place Where Encounter Can Occur

At the Beginning, a *Presence*

Respect is to be understood here in the sense of a "contemplative respect," for it implies a way of being in relationship that only union with Christ can make possible. In this sense, it substitutes for the term "adoration," but its origin is the same. In other words, "it is a new respect that is born from a personal relationship with Christ."[227] And this elicits a certain reticence because such an experience is hardly ordinary. On the contrary, it stands out in a most extraordinary way. To quote Emmanuel Lévinas,

---

227 Society of the Sacred Heart, *1976 General Chapter*, Rome, p. 9.

it is "the marvel of Presence coming to us from the heights."[228] To communicate such an experience can hardly make use of worn out, emotionally charged words without undercutting and thus betraying it. The fact is that certain realities, through the overabundance of their source, elude any attempt to explain or conceptualize them. Such is the case with the word "heart," used to express the charism of union and conformity with the Heart of Christ,[229] or the invitation to "rest in his love."[230]

On this topic, the theologian Karl Rahner recommended using the term "Heart of Christ" with discretion and counseled "using it only when it is a question of designating a person engaged in the most intimate and secret place of his being, when engaged with Jesus Christ, whether through his immeasurable plenitude, or through ourselves, in view of how this dispersion fills our emptiness." And he adds: "This happens only rarely; but it carries with it enormous importance. Consider the Lord himself. It is rarely, but always during decisive moments, that he speaks from his heart to ours."[231] The biblical metaphor of the river, in the previously mentioned letters, corresponds closely to one of those moments in the sense that the founding symbol has found the biblical landscape that allowed it to become "living"—in other words, to stimulate collective creativity and evangelical dynamism.

---

228 E. Lévinas, *Totalité et Infinité*, Martinus Nijhoff Publishers, La Haye, 1980, p. 59.

229 The spiritual tradition of the French School uses the expressions "interior dispositions of the Heart of Christ" or "interior of Christ," which pose the same difficulties.

230 *Letters to the Society,* Concepción Camacho, Letter 5 of June 18, 1971, p. 10. Letter 16 of June 21, 1974, p. 39.

231 K. Rahner, *Mission et Grâce*, vol. III, Mame, Paris, 1965, p. 251.

An educational priority flowed from this: to foster conditions that would allow people to experience divine transcendence and thus become aware of the grandeur of the human person called to participate in divine life and its radiance. The 1982 Constitutions expressed it in terms of the first insights: "We unite our desire with that of Saint Madeleine Sophie, awakened to truth and love and liberty, to discover the meaning of life and share it with others, to play her creative part in the transformation of the world, to thereby encounter the love of Jesus, to commit herself to an active faith."[232]

In 1988 this orientation was restated in the form of a recommendation: "Be particularly attentive to those young people most seriously wounded... by poverty, violence, pressure from competition, drug addiction, AIDS, emigration, family break-up, etc.... so that they can discover their own dignity and find their place in life."[233] If respect reveals the image that one has of other people or cultures, a key characteristic of it here is to call everyone to liberty and responsibility—to an expansion of life, whatever the uncertainties of personal or collective history.

The Sacred Heart schools in Spain formulated it this way:
- To ensure that students ask themselves the fundamental question of life's meaning in order that they arrive at an understanding of God as mystery and orient their life around this perspective, from the standpoint of an unending search for truth.

---

232 *Notre service d'Eglise*, 11., p. 171.
233 *1988 General Chapter*, Orientation #4, Rome, p. 12.

- To form people capable of hope, opening up horizons for them in order that they might interpret reality from the perspective of Christian values, and stimulating openness to the world through knowledge of the love of Jesus Christ and his message."[234]

Awakeners of Meaning

In 1988, the spiritual goal was translated in terms of objectives: "to introduce the power of the Gospel to young people, to discover with them how to incarnate the Gospel in every part of their lives." Thus, "transformed by the experience of God and the discovery of such communities, filled with a new appetite for life, these youths will become evangelizers of others." They become missionaries, carriers of the living water. It is an essential question for both youths and adults, one with a single and identical purpose: to announce the merciful love of God through a variety of encounters, to awaken "a new appetite for life."

This challenge emerges out of the contemporary belief that life has no meaning. "Godlessness," which motivated the original plan of Sophie Barat, today takes the form of indifference to religion or of nihilism. In the face of such a challenge, the response must be radical: Christ, "the Word made flesh," has "come in order to dwell in a world which is searching for the meaning and true value of life."[235] It is thus a question of collaborating with the work of Jesus Christ himself. Such an engagement does not take place on its own. The ability to choose one's own life arises out of the act of adoration: "Only the consideration of

---

[234] *Caractère propre des Collèges du Sacré Coeur*, Madrid 1997, A. S-C. ES., p. 10.

[235] Société du Sacré-Cœur, *Constitutions de 1982*, #41., Rome, p. 183.

people and events in the light of prayer can impel us to take our part in building a more human world, and to feel the urgency of its needs."[236]

Contemplative respect, of course, describes a relationship with three slightly imbalanced elements. An unconditional openness, evidence of the active presence of the Transcendent, is also the foundation of hope, living water for our time. According to this spiritual tradition, the educational relationship is not on the order of "I-Thou," as many contemporary anthropologists would argue. The founding charism cannot be practiced unless it involves the process and otherness of an encounter occurring at the dual level of human reality and the Word of God. Today it assumes the image of an emblem. In accordance with the figure of the servant Christ, characteristics of vulnerability and reciprocity, of compassion and solidarity, emerge, replacing the virtues of Julien Druilhet's portrait of a "child of the Sacred Heart." Such an approach leads to a commitment that envisions greater social justice and "allows God to become visible."[237]

Gratuity as Golden Rule

In assuming the face of gratuity, the educational relationship reveals that which it makes possible: the Completely-Other. However, as this expression indicates, the Transcendent is neither definable nor locatable. In this case, we might even say that It emerges out of the "non-place." However, it is precisely this ontological break that comes together with an unconditional

---

[236] *Letters to the Society,* Concepción Camacho, Lettre 1, November 28 1970, p. 1.

[237] *Letters to the Society,* Concepción Camacho, Letter 23, November 14 1976, p. 56.

openness of exchange and identifies it with the golden rule: a gratuitous love that runs through history in order to make "all things new."[238] Every form of violence shatters in the face of it, from the slightest to the most offensive: See oneself as another or seek to destroy him.[239]

From contemplation comes, too, the capacity to forgive. Biblical wisdom qualifies this attitude of gratuity and freedom in this way: "neither a lender nor a borrower be". For this reason, brotherly love, under the varying forms of service, esteem, and friendship, cannot be lived simply as "a duty" but as "a grace."[240]

Where tradition spoke of simplicity, a lively faith, and missionary zeal, today's documents summon us to evangelization and mutual liberation. If the language has changed, the meaning is the same. It is a matter of Good News to be shared: to create a new way of being in the world. To act with gratuity in order to allow the other to rediscover his self-esteem, to value one another within these assumed responsibilities, is "to glorify Christ." To reveal the immeasurable force of his tenderness and forgiveness is another. In either case, it is a question of respecting the other—at the heart of his or her misery as well as his or her fulfillment.

It was this way of being and acting that the Institute, according to its spirituality, sought to form in its students. Indeed, the General Chapter of 1994 made it a course of action: "The search for reconciliation and peace calls us to develop methodologies

---

238 This expression can be found in Letter 12, December 15, 1972, p. 29.

239 See Paul Ricœur, *Soi-même comme un autre*, Seuil, Paris, 1990, p. 256 to 258. [Tr. note: a key aspect of Ricœur's philosophy considers understanding others as a means to understanding oneself.]

240 *Letters to the Society,* Concepción Camacho, Letter 27, August 4 1977, p. 66.

based on non-violence, to foster relationships where there is participation and reciprocity."[241] Is it not to this perfection of love that Christianity calls us? For the sole reason that we are made in the image of God whose Love is freely given?

The presence of divine transcendence thus works in favor of every possible interaction, without reducing or minimizing the other person. Today, as in the past, a quality of respect allows for some uprootedness at the heart of such encounters, in order to create educational responses adapted to specific situations and persons.

In the same way, the social purpose cannot be separated from the spiritual goal. "To accomplish justice" requires both. The regenerative grace present in every reality is a freely given gift received from the open side of Christ. Thus, "day after day, the Eucharist allows us to become, more and more deeply, the Body of Christ given up so that a new humanity might be born."[242] In effect, according to the missionary theology of Paul, grace is associated with the Eucharist and with a justice whose meaning is to "render effective the freely given gift." This is why the social purpose of the Society of the Sacred Heart is inseparable from its spiritual goal. It is also why a course of action might easily take several different forms in terms of compassion, solidarity, liberation and reconciliation. While the expressions might vary according to the situations and the socio-political challenges, the paradigm is the same: communion. To act in this way is to do nothing more than to accomplish "the justice of Christ."[243]

---

241 Society of the Sacred Heart, 1994 General Chapter, Rome, p. 16.

242 Société du Sacré-Cœur de Jésus, *Constitutions de 1982, Notre prière*, 29, p. 178.

243 *Letters to the Society,* Concepción Camacho, Letter 12, Dec. 15, 1972, p. 28.

This interweaving of the two parameters "grace-justice" within one educational goal can be seen throughout the framework of the educational plan in Latin America and the Caribbean. It is expressed through a constellation of phrases: "gratuity of creation," "overabundance of grace," "passage into the light," "justice and gift freely offered," "reconciliation," "the power of liberation through an individual and a collective process," "a passion to announce the Gospel incarnate in the research into a new social and ethical order." This series of "motifs" unfolds against a typical missionary horizon: a landscape in which human dignity is often usurped or violated. This scourge results from an economic model that is "dehumanizing and corrupt, where money has become the measure of everything, and where the weakest are excluded." It might be combated, however, through the missionary effectiveness of the Sacred Heart schools. The proposed model is Philippine Duchesne, who invites us to construct a more humane world in which wealth is more evenly divided.

This goal is accomplished in various ways, depending on the country and the forms of educational intervention. The province of Peru chose to work toward the revaluing of Andean, Amazonian, and grassroots cultures, and toward reconciliation among Peruvians. Up against an economic system that, from their point of view, destroys solidarity, dismantles organizations, and establishes authoritarian relationships, it opted to collaborate on a variety of projects, such as that of Bambamarca, in the province of Cajamarca.[244] One plan of action involved women in the countryside, with the goal to "confront the serious

---

244 *Orientations pour la marche des institutions éducatives du Sacré-Cœur au Pérou*, A. S-C, PER, p. 1.

problems that affect them: poverty, illiteracy, marginalization, etc."²⁴⁵ At the Alcides Vasquez Center, the project sought to create future leaders of grassroots communities. Several objectives were defined: "to support and enliven a critical and self-critical sense; to fight to defend the interests of small farmers and their organizations; and to maintain and defend the rural customs, traditions, and riches of the Andean reality."²⁴⁶

The province of Mexico took a similar route. It wanted to fight the deterioration of the social climate afflicting the countryside and the poverty that affected, in particular, women, children, marginalized youth, indigenous peoples, and university students.²⁴⁷

The same held true at the St. Julian School in Malta. The educational plan aimed to form citizens of a non-violent world in a Christian manner. A number of social projects were proposed, aimed at combating injustice and promoting ecological progress.

These various objectives were gathered up into a single statement found in paragraphs 13 and 15 of the 1982 Constitutions: "Whatever our work may be, our lives will be inspired by the love of the Heart of Jesus and the desire of making Him known, expressed in: a concern for growth of the whole person; a thirst for working towards justice and peace in the world in response to the cry of the poor; a passion to proclaim the Gospel." This

---

245 *Petit projet pour les femmes de la campagne de Bambamarca, département de Cajamarca, Pérou*, A. S-C. PER, p. 1-2.

246 *Expérience du Centre d'adultes "Alcides Vasquez" pour la formation des paysans*, A. S-C. PER, p. 1.

247 Province of Mexico, *Apport de l'éducation populaire au projet apostolique commun*, A. S-C, MXN., p. 4.

fundamental change of real situations is referred to today as "education for justice in faith."

A Hope of Communicating to All Nations

Divine Otherness also provides an opening into numerous cultural spaces. It is the keystone of the universal dimension that characterizes different forms of education within the Society of the Sacred Heart. In terms of formal education, internationality is lived in a number of ways: student exchange programs, linguistic and cultural experiences for students, exchanges and collaboration between educational teams. In 1980, an international network was established among Sacred Heart schools. To the existing linguistic exchanges were added sports and artistic competitions. The objectives were the following:
- to recognize that we belong to a reality far larger than that of our own schools;
- to expand students' abilities to relate with one another in a multicultural, multiracial world;

- to bring alive the meaning of competition;
- to promote exchanges between students of different countries, languages, and cultures and discover one another's distinctiveness and riches;
- to develop an awareness of the challenges present in today's globalization.

The directors of this network, consisting of two hundred Sacred Heart schools or universities, met regularly by country, by region, or by continent in order to reflect on their responsibility. Thus, in 1998 in Latin America and the Caribbean, the educational communities of ten countries drafted a common educational plan.[248] And in April 2000, eighty-nine directors of Sacred Heart schools from five continents gathered in Joigny. They wrote this declaration: "We wish to live our internationality as 'good news' for the poor, and in this intention we commit ourselves to seek together, within our educational institutions, ways to establish projects that promote more solidarity, communion, and peace education."

Openness to the all-embracing took other forms, no less promising, within popular education. In some of places, it was a question of constructing connections among ethnicities, races, and cultures. The goal was to offer a way to cross borders in a spirit of generosity and charity, to connect differences at the heart of the familiar. Thus, in the midst of a Brazilian forest, Elisabeth Amarante lived for 24 years among the Myky, following

---

248 "*El espiritu educador del Sagrado Corazón en las instituciones de América latina y el Caraibe*," Lima, 1-8 October 1998.

their customs.²⁴⁹ And she campaigned through an association to defend the rights of indigenous people.

On another continent, in the Uganda-Kenya province, the educators aimed to awaken in young women a sense of their dignity and worth, their human rights, and the possibility of relationships with other ethnicities. The same thing occurred in Chad, near Bongor, where the *Center for the Future of Guelengdeng*²⁵⁰ was created for the advancement of women. There again, the approach recalled the intrepidity of the pioneers of the Society's beginnings in that understanding came through immersion in the local environment. In 1985, Marie-Thérèse Kabalu Kantshiama, a Congolese, went to live for two months in a Masa family. As she learned the rudiments of the Masa language, she also discovered that segregation confined women to menial work, to the kitchen, to the transporting of wood. Not knowing how to count, read or write, these young women often found themselves cheated. In order to avoid this, they were encouraged to learn to read, count and write. A concerted action allowed them to communicate further among themselves and their neighboring tribes in order to escape an alienating supervision, and to free themselves from ancestral rules of confinement. A first literacy group was thus established to create bridges between ethnic groups and to study the fundamentals of arithmetic and language.

The starting point for these exchanges was a reading from

---

249 The Myky people of Brazil have had no contact with whites until the past 30 years.

250 The educational activity of the RSCJ can be found in the orientations for development (agriculture, health, advancement of women) taken by the diocese of Pala in Chad, over the past 20 years.

Book 24 of Matthew's Gospel. From this shared experience, the group received its name: *Min Tuvuda* (Mamas of Charity) as well as its goals: to visit the sick; to help one another; to participate in familial events. Reunions also took place in other villages, including those of the Masa, Marba, Toupouri, Mosey, and the like. In three years, three hundred women had entered this movement of mutual aid between villages and ethnic groups. And just as traditional culture reinforces behavior through imitation of one's elders, so, too, this movement resulted in introducing the education of girls. In response to those who had expressed a desire for it, a sewing and embroidery workshop was created. It was in this way that, in 1987, a plan for a girls' school was created at the *Center for the Future of Guelengdeng*.

These concrete forms of interdependence were facilitated by the international and multicultural character of the Society of the Sacred Heart.[251] They are also thriving on other continents. Thus, in 1998, in Biscaye, Spain, the Center of Urbinaga developed a project of popular education with the following goals: to create a place of intercultural friendliness, dialogue and solidarity; to develop a communal attitude and an awareness of the neighborhood in order to improve the quality of life.

In India, several projects might also serve as illustration. In Mumbai, Sophia College's Polytechnic school is considered a leader in technical education in Maharashtra. This school contributes to the promotion and valuing of women by providing them with a professional competency—a measure of heightened economic power. Founded in 1970, it has prepared over 25,000 young adults, mostly women; in the junior school

---

251 Society of the Sacred Heart, General Chapter, 1988, Rome, p. 13-14.

and university, one finds courses on building awareness of discrimination against women within the Indian social system and ways to combat it. In the Northeastern area of Jawhar Taluka, the Religious of the Sacred Heart run pilot projects in support of women belonging to the Zilla Parishad ethnic group, projects that are subsidized by UNESCO. And in Haregaon, the Saint Theresa School addressed especially the needs of young Catholic girls confronted by poverty and the discriminations of caste. In the same way, at the Sadhana School in Mumbai, a pioneer project was established for autistic children, following the methods of Bérard.[252]

All of these actions concretize a key orientation of the Society of the Sacred Heart: to be open to the universal; to create spaces within which personal and cultural identities are respected and, if possible, validated.

III.2 A Pathway, to Discern in Order to Accomplish Justice

The Book of Proverbs links two kinds of activities: discernment and the carrying out of justice. One does not exist without the other: "Yes, if you cry out for discernment, and lift up your voice for understanding, if you seek her as silver, and search for her as for hidden treasures; then you will understand ... the knowledge of God, you will understand justice, equity, every good path;

---

252 Tr. Note: The SPJ Sadhana School today serves the needs of students with a variety of developmental challenges: "With an experience of 41 years S.P.J. Sadhana School ... has been working ceaselessly towards training the mentally challenged by not only helping them to be productive members of society but also making them independent and self-sufficient." http://www.spjsadhanaschool.org/about-us/

the only path that leads to happiness."[253] This understanding is wisdom: it opens up horizons that are capable of giving meaning to life and fostering the art of living an evangelical life.

Learning to Discern with a View toward Commitment
In the course of renewing their work of education, the Religious of the Sacred Heart had recourse to discernment so often that it became an incontrovertible rule, the new "integrating principle" of every educational step. Such an emphasis was new: affirmed collectively in 1970, it can be found in all subsequent documents. Rhetoric was no longer the preferred method for evangelizing influential social milieus by means of the Humanities. It was supplanted by a "little light" that, in a secularized world, enabled one's actions to be guided by the Gospel.

In 1970, discernment called for to implement the second option of the General Chapter: "To aim at the development of a faith capable of taking on a secularized world, a serious esteem for intellectual values, and education with a social sense that compels to action." The goal was the development of the whole person. And discernment was selected as the way to assure the development of personal wholeness and professional choices.

This unifying activity is pointed out in the first part of the 1976 document entitled *Charism, Facilitator of Unity, Continuity, and Change*. Charism was characterized and developed along three lines: contemplation, communion, and education. As the following diagram shows, the educational mission is centered on a struggle for justice:

---

253 Book of Proverbs 2:1-9.

Subordinated to the achievement of justice and solidarity—aspects of communion and fraternity—discernment is a needed intermediary.

On May 25, 1977, Concepción Camacho invited her sisters to live this requirement in relating an experience she underwent in Joigny:

> Looking at the simple, calm, serene countryside that Madeleine Sophie so often contemplated, I grew in understanding of the simplicity that she wished for our spirituality, and of the serenity of one who lives by faith. I felt and tasted the pulse of that spirituality, centered in love, its power of interiority, leading us to contemplate the Lord and to recognize him in all things. . . . It is God who urges us "to be one with men in their sufferings and in their quest for a more just and fraternal world"—without compromising with its values which are contrary to the Gospel, without identifying ourselves with the world.[254]

---

[254] *Letters to the Society,* Concepción Camacho, Letter 26, May 25, 1977, p. 63.

This art of living involves the work of discernment.[255]

The Constitutions of 1982 confirmed the Society's educational purpose: to educate students to "a broad critical vision of the world, enlightened by faith."[256] Many educational undertakings chose it for an ultimate goal. Within the corpus of works examined, this unifying rule calls for a variety of goals. A partial list includes the following: to be conscious of one's dignity; to feel oneself to be a child of God; to discover or rediscover a personal and cultural identity; to promote acknowledgement of equality between men and women, within their differences; to access a new esteem for oneself and others; to develop critical thinking and a moral and political conscience; to discover a meaning to life; to commit oneself; to be creative; to work with others in order to transform society.

Whatever the target population, progress involved pairing personal integration and commitment. The methods and means used to carry out these educational principles adapted themselves to the people and groups in question. As was the case "at the time of the Society's beginnings," scientific and technological discoveries were there to serve a spiritual goal: to enable one to recognize the presence of God in history.

For Sophie Barat, to reach this goal meant developing the kind of thinking that characterized the humanities curriculum. Today, to recognize basic otherness at work in the world requires the ability to discern. Its ongoing acquisition should underlie

---

255 *Letters to the Society,* Concepción Camacho, Letter 8, p. 17.
256 1982 Constitutions, *Service in the Church,* 14, p. 172.

curriculum development. It is always a question of charting one's own "pathway," to choose with wisdom and foresight those plans and the means to realize them. It was thus that the Mexico-Nicaragua Province aimed to educate young people and women capable of reflection and expression, of decision and critical thinking, of solidarity with the poor. The same thing held true for many other provinces. To develop the intelligence with a view toward thinking for oneself and living one's life according to the Gospel remained the educational priority of the Institute.

With this goal in mind, in Japan, at the University of the Sacred Heart in Tokyo, an exchange program was established in 1985 with schools in the Philippines. The students lived with families so that they were able to experience and feel the cultural and religious differences, to witness the profound faith of those who live in poverty, and to reflect on their own faith. Surprised by the humor and vitality of the people living in slums, these students began to question their own way of life and their values. In the educational plan of the Society's "beginnings," the course on astronomical geography stimulated this kind of questioning. Today, it is immersion in a "foreign land," in the manner of Philippine Duchesne, that brings forth this kind of self-questioning. Cultural shock can provoke challenge and discernment with a view toward future undertakings.

This pedagogical method appears in many Sacred Heart educational projects. It is present in the United States, described earlier, in the form of humanitarian action.[257] It is seen in France under the form of small

---

[257] The same applies to educational projects undertaken in the provinces of Australia-New Zealand, and Austria-Hungary, following the model of those in the U.S.

projects, such as action taken by students at the school in Amiens on behalf of Chadians in the neighborhood of Chagwa, N'Djamena, for several summers in a row. It has also been chosen for the training of future teachers at the National Institute of Monterrico, in Peru.[258] Students participate in educational activities for homeless children and orphans. In Chile, young university students belonging to the Ignatian movement CLC (Christian Life Community) offer their legal and psychological skills to people who live in the impoverished neighborhoods of Paricanota.

In this way, the young acquire the ability to communicate and work with people from different circumstances. They learn to respect other cultures and other religions, and to develop strong relationships.

To Walk Humbly, Making a Path Together

The "Attitudes in View of Mission" determined in 1976 marked an unequivocal shift in the way of life for the Religious of the Sacred Heart. It consisted less of "knowing" than it did seeking together. To proximity were joined reciprocity and solidarity. From now on, the watchword was "humbly, and with courage, together, we walk the same way."[259]

In 1988, the priorities moved intentionally toward "those

---

258 Founded in 1857, this teachers college in Monterrico is still run by Religious of the Sacred Heart.

259 Society of the Sacred Heart of Jesus, *1988 General Chapter, Solidarity with the Poor,* p. 22.

who, in many cultures, live with inequality and even oppression."[260] The relationship skills contributed to "the healing of wounds, and to educating to love and responsibility." Four starting points were chosen:

	young people	
those who are poor		migrants
	women	

With respect to young people, it meant being especially attentive to the most wounded to seek solutions to their situation with them; to propose specific ways to help them find their dignity and place in life.

With the poor and migrants, it involved appreciating the worth of their respective cultures and religions; developing possible solutions to their problems through serious analyses, made with others and especially with the poor themselves; questioning the coherence of possible choices.

With women, it meant raising awareness of the value of human life. And in the face of challenges concerning procreation, they had to become informed about current research, the services that new technology could provide, and the consequences that these might have for the human person.

In every case, it meant finding a framework of cooperation so that small-scale projects of solidarity and service could be sought out together. To this type of educational or formational accompaniment corresponded an understanding of the person to which we have already made reference. Its essential

---

260 *Introduction to the General Chapter Report*, p. 9.

component was the "absolute dignity" of all. The human person is seen as a being of possibility, capable of personal integration, autonomy and responsibility, of social engagement, and creativity. Autonomy and responsibility encircle the gift of the Gospel's message; they surround solidarity and service with the goal of promoting justice and peace through social change.

Such a missionary challenge naturally brought with it an evolution in the designs and methods of educational practice. The institutional challenge, identified in 1967, was to respond to the crises of values in the contemporary world. The collaborative approach to reinterpreting the founding charism resulted in its reaffirmation. To liberate and heal, to rebuild what has been destroyed, to reconcile what has been divided, are equal expressions of a single educational vision—to accomplish justice, the contemporary expression for the *primordial idea of the little society*: to create a spirit of adoration and reparation.

III.3 In Memory of the Covenant

Various kinds of educational responses convey an evangelical message for our time, a hope for communication in a world where transcendence has been obscured. Divine is found there as both "principle and end."[261] The book of Revelation expresses it in an original way: "I am the Alpha and the Omega, the Principle and the End; to all who are thirsty, I will give freely from the springs of the water of life."[262] To receive this gift is to reawaken to a new way of being in the world.

---

261 Following the wording of the *Spiritual Exercises* of Ignatius Loyola.
262 Revelation, 21, 6.

Educators are thus associated with a mission that extends far beyond them. But one's capacity to engage in building a more just society derives from the strength of Christ's resurrection. This transcendent condition is reaffirmed regularly as the key reference point for every educational project, whose function is as much to guide as it is to question.

When Renewal is Accomplishment

Today like yesterday, the task is to impart wisdom, to give meaning to the Gospel's message. The frame of reference for studying any text is the Covenant of God and God's people. The symbol of the Covenant was the underpinning for the religion program in the first Plan of Studies and was the organizing principle for the entire curriculum. During the process of renewal, it was set forth is a metaphor newly brought to life. It is thus not surprising that it appeared in the 1982 Constitutions, in the first paragraph of the article on Service in the Church: "We are sent by the Church to communicate the love of the Heart of Jesus. In Him all find their true growth as persons and the way towards reconciliation with one another."[263]

The foregoing discussion has pointed to the source of the metaphor of the river, essential to the spirituality of the Society of the Sacred Heart: that of an encounter, of an experience to be communicated. The goal is to prepare students, through education, for a personal encounter with Christ—to emphasize those intellectual and pastoral conditions necessary for it to happen. This priority appears in the textual framework under several

---

263 Society of the Sacred Heart of Jesus, *1982 Constitutions*, p. 10, Rome.

headings: spiritual intuition – source of conversion – power of transformation – witnessing – living water to communicate.

This paradigm is obviously not limited to the Society of the Sacred Heart; it constitutes the framework for any Christian discourse. However, the central motif around which the institutional culture is organized is unique: the image of the "open Side of Jesus," associated with a privileged link to the Eucharistic symbol. It is a question of contributing "to the evolution of communion in Christ" through the work of education.

The Eucharist derives its particular purpose from allowing us to "enter into the mystery of the open side of Jesus," to celebrate and actualize "his death and resurrection, the reality which lies at the heart of the sufferings and hopes of the human family."[264] This purpose is likewise made clear in terms of re-birth: "Gradually, the Eucharist makes us become more truly the Body of Christ, broken to give birth to a new humanity."[265] This particular connection involves a spiritual energy through which both contemplation and a freeing process signal, according to the figure of Christ suggested, a way of life marked by "the adoration of the Father" and "service to the human family, particularly the poor."

Today's educational challenge is without doubt an expansion of the challenge understood by Sophie Barat. Various forms of violence continue to divide social groups and nations. But globalization and the deadly technological means now at our disposal have radicalized the contemporary challenge. The risks

---

264 Society of the Sacred Heart of Jesus, *1982 Constitutions*, 5.
265 Society of the Sacred Heart of Jesus, *1982 Constitutions, Prayer*, 29.

are no longer simply personal or national—they are capable of affecting the integrity of the entire planet. It is thus at a new, global level that we must find solutions that are worthy of the human being—the image of Christ. The Society of the Sacred Heart desires to contribute to such a solution by preparing citizens in nonviolence, men and women who will usher in Christ's wisdom.

The hope to be shared is the mystery of the Covenant. It might be called a regenerated communion, powerfully conveyed by the biblical image of "the river that flows through history." This communion is of the order of the "already here" and of the "not yet." It calls forth, at one and the same time, the action of grace and of commitment.

An Open Table

Written in poetic form, a passage from the General Chapter of 1994 interprets in an unforeseen way "the essential idea" of Sophie Barat. It is entitled "The Eucharistic Dimension of Our Spirituality"[266] and develops around a central idea: "to revive hope and keep it alive."

It directly references Christ by means of two Gospel references:

> *I have compassion on these people. . . .*
> *Give them something to eat (Mark 6:37).*
> *I have come that they may have life*
> *and have it in abundance (John 10:10).*

Next, the founding symbol is inscribed into the framework

---

[266] Society of the Sacred Heart, *1994 General Chapter*, 1994, Rome, p. 27 to 31.

of the poem:
> *We feel a new strength*
> *coming from our spirituality,*
> *as a movement of the Spirit*
> *which springs from the **open side of Christ**,*
> *a dynamism*
> *an inspiration*
> *a fire*
> *which can transform and transfigure our lives*
> *and give us a prophetic vision of the world.*

The place of adoration has become the political stage, the world of educational activity, where "the beauty of our earth, the ecological crisis, the dignity and weight of human work" beckon and call out to us. Within our contemporary reality, it is a question of keeping in mind "the remembrance of what Jesus did: as a gift of life to others."

By means of this living memory, educators are brought back to the everyday world, "ready to nourish life, weaving relationships of trust and communion, creating a space where life can flourish." But the true participants in the revelation of the "face of God of tenderness and mercy" are the poor, the marginalized, and the victims of violence. It is they who "call us together to live Eucharist as reconciliation."

In this way, the event being commemorated is today's event. In order to enter into it—that is to say, to seat ourselves at the table of guests—the required condition is "to be reborn, to welcome grace." But a surprise is waiting for us. Added to the traditional recipients of educational service is a guest of honor: "all of creation." The seating at the table is wide open.

Several passages illustrate this scenario:
> Hope impels us
> to try to make of our world
> a great banquet
> an open table
> where both bread and word are shared
> where Christ wipes away the tears of so much oppression,
> injustice, violence, division.
> What draws us together
> is the celebration of the daughters and sons of God
> where the little ones are the first
> and where we wash one another's feet
> weary from the journey.
>
> All of our reality
> personal,
> communal,
> apostolic
> finds integration there
> and becomes eucharistic.
> Madeleine Sophie's vision of adoration
> invites us to enter into the thoughts of God
> "which remain from age to age
> to save their lives from death
> and to give them life in time of famine" (Ps 32: 11-19).
>
> Living and celebrating the Eucharist
> through the light and shadow of daily life
> becomes one single movement.
> The Spirit reveals the presence of Christ

both in the Sacrament
and the world that suffers and waits in hope.

The movement of adoration is visible within the dynamic of the poem. Before each encountered reality, for each guest at the banquet, it cites an evangelical element and echoes the values, present in the encounter as well as the language.

In this way, the creative image is brought to life. Two hundred years earlier, before a "solitary tabernacle," young Sophie imagined it as "a crowd of adorers before a universal monstrance." In 1994, a new image of the Eucharistic banquet was the work of the whole Society.

The stage is international. Within this dimension, fitting for the place education occupies in the Society of the Sacred Heart, emerges the call to "overcome the difficulties, to confront differences," to "recognize" a transformative action at work within different cultures. It calls up a worldwide vision, that of "rendering our earth habitable for all, without exclusion," to care for all of creation.

Social commitment takes on here the face of compassion and solidarity with those whose lives are "torn and broken by the injustices of the world." Education, the work of liberation and reconciliation shaped in the light of the Covenant, is in a single act a restoration of the image of oneself and others, rebirth, announcement of Good News, and shared bread.

To take time for interiority in order to be visited by Another, to be capable of finding means that extend beyond the normal hopes of the possible. That is what this poem evokes: through the sharing of a bit of bread and some fish; to nourish an enormous crowd; to form followers who will announce through their actions the face of tenderness and the liberating force of Christ Jesus, this promise "of love for all," to be communicated "to all nations."

CONCLUSION

New Challenges, Living Water to Be Shared

DRAWING ON TWO SIGNIFICANT MOMENTS in the history of the Society of the Sacred Heart of Jesus—its founding and its renewal—this study has described specific elements of an educational tradition and a way of being in the world.

These constraints are represented by the image of birth. An innovative choice, it characterizes the original undertaking in its legal form, in its goals, and above all in the initiative that created it. The form was spelled out by Léonor de Tournély; the goal, elaborated by Sophie Barat; the social purpose, defined by both. However, the nature of the experience out of which the creative intuition sprang is fundamental. For the Institute's earliest participants, this novelty sprang from the contemplation of Christ as he was present in the real world. This means that the regenerative power of the resurrected Christ came to them during the act of adoration; while they were considering their contemporary needs, they were receiving the project from Another. The source of the image is this transcendent reality "that makes all things new." The capacity to transform social reality or to reconcile oneself with one's own personal or collective history comes to us from Christ the Servant.

From this initial experience, the missionary purpose takes its expression and its shape. For Father Druilhet, the vocation of the "children of the Sacred Heart" was to "cause religion to be reborn from its ashes." To combat godlessness, to construct a solid foundation for a living and responsive faith, to rebuild the social fabric according to Christian values—these were some of its expressions, like so many subjects on a single canvas. In this time of globalization, the effects of social and personal disintegration emerge from causes far more complex than those of the French Revolution. The phenomenon is not specific to a particular nation or people; it has worldwide reach. And while differing in kind and scope, it affects every stratum of the human population.

These new appeals stimulate other kinds of action. But, today like yesterday, the educational goal is the same: to allow students to recognize their individuality, to discover life's meaning, and to behave in light of this awareness. Education is centered on the discovery of human dignity and its transcendence. In the nineteenth century, with the understanding that nature is directed to a final cause, the pedagogical means of understanding the cosmos arose from the Humanities, conceived according to the model of the Jesuits' *Ratio studiorum*. In the twenty-first century, in a time of globalization and in a world of many human cultures, educating to spiritual discernment with a view toward promoting a more humane society must be developed and pursued beyond purely scholarly frameworks.

In this sense, returning to the sources of the Society of the Sacred Heart takes us all the way back to Ignatius Loyola, as

Sophie allows him to be understood in the *Journal of Poitiers*.[267] Thereafter, the methods and content of education had to be adapted to its recipients, and to the kind of educational measures being undertaken. But, then and now, following the lead of the educators at the "beginnings" means "being reborn to a way of loving Christ."

The institutional priorities favor the vulnerable, in particular youth and women, and persons whose identity and dignity have been wounded by injustice. The "farthest away" culturally is the "nearest," as is the object of God's preference, and an openness to new forms of educational measures reflects the worldwide within the immediacy of place.

Thus, in connection with different situations, the biblical metaphor of the river of living water continues to unleash its power. The many concepts embodied in this metaphor enable its broad application. Whatever the socio-political landscape or language used to deepen the distinctive ethic, the components of all the projects center on one theme: justice within love. In the educational activity and institutional choices, educators must make visible the "hidden mystery" of the liberating action of Christ and communicate its sense of hope.

The term *justice*, present in the formation to adoration that was Sophie's goal from the beginning, is now to be understood at an ontological level as the expansion of the original educational project. The biblical referent is the word of Christ uttered at his baptism on the shores of the Jordan River: "I am come to

---

[267] "The great Saint whose spirit we wish to follow judged otherwise," *Sainte Madeleine-Sophie Barat, Journal de Poitiers*, text presented by M.-T. Virnot, Reprint Ligugé, 1977, A. S-C, Rome.

fulfill all justice."[268] In other words, it means allowing human beings to rediscover the source of their "glorious" humanity in a way that allows them to be "returned" to themselves in their first identity, knowing themselves loved by God and capable of working with others to create a more humane society.

In the Society of the Sacred Heart, the ethical goal consists of stimulating this act of rebirth, of ontological "restoration" in communication and in action, and of finding the means to enact it. To train responsible women and men, able to share their convictions and act in accordance with Gospel values in order to transform society: such is, in fact, the goal of every educational activity. The missionary idea of nearness and distance is engraved on the international institutional horizon, facilitating cultural exchanges, formative experiences, and acts of solidarity.

Against a backdrop of esteem and compassion, an inexhaustible Goodness must make itself known in the outlook and actions of every educator. It is a call to grow through interaction with those most deprived of resources. To awaken in the other this inwardness against a backdrop of liberty and transcendence: such is the unique and multifaceted mission to which are called those who, within their networks of collaboration and sharing, are collaborators in this educational ethic.

---

268 Matthew 3:15.

Bibilography

Note: As most of the secondary sources for this book are available only in French, we include here a sampling of recent works in English that offer further information about the Society of the Sacred Heart and its educational philosophy and history.

Gimber, Frances, RSCJ, *Saint Madeleine Sophie Barat (1779-1865) Founder of the Society of the Sacred Heart of Jesus*, Society of the Sacred Heart, United States-Canada, St. Louis, 2024

Kilroy, Phil, RSCJ, *Madeleine Sophie Barat: A Life*, Cork University Press, Cork, 2000

Luirard, Monique, RSCJ, *The Society of the Sacred Heart in the World of Its Times 1865-2000*, Society of the Sacred Heart, United States-Canada, St. Louis, 2016

Maxwell, Susan Putman, RSCJ, *Times Change: A History of the Network of Sacred Heart Schools*, Society of the Sacred Heart, United States-Canada, St. Louis, 2017

Osiek, Carolyn, RSCJ, *Saint Philippine Duchesne: A Heart on Fire across Frontiers*, Society of the Sacred Heart, United States-Canada, St. Louis, 2017

Goals and Criteria: Sacred Heart Schools United States and Canada, Society of the Sacred Heart, United States-Canada, St. Louis, 2020

Philippine Duchesne: Pioneer on the America Frontier (1769-1852) Complete Works, Editors: Marie-France Carreel, RSCJ, and Carolyn Osiek, RSCJ, Brepols Publishers, Turnhout, Belgium, 2019

Sophie's Gift: Philosophy of Sacred Heart Education, International Education Commission, Rome, 2023

Transformed: One Congregation's Response to the Second Vatican Council and the Calls of the World, Editors: Bonnie Kearney, RSCJ, and Diane Roche, RSCJ, Society of the Sacred Heart, United States-Canada, St. Louis, 2023

Besides print materials, see: www.sacredheartusc.education

Society of the Sacred Heart™
United States – Canada

rscj.org/news/publications

FOLLOW US

facebook.com/SocietyoftheSacredHeart
facebook.com/ReligiousOfTheSacredHeart (Vocations)
instagram.com/_societyofthesacredheart
vimeo.com/rscjusc
linkedin.com/company/society-of-the-sacred-heart-usc

Network of Sacred Heart Schools
www.sacredheartusc.education
instagram.com/networkofshschools

www.ingramcontent.com/pod-product-compliance
Lightning Source LLC
Chambersburg PA
CBHW042320090526
44585CB00024BA/2660